MW00323898

# THROUGH A
# SPARKLING GLASS

Andrea Frost

# THE AUTHOR

An award-winning wine writer with a passion and curiosity for the wonder of wine, Andrea is the wine columnist for *delicious* magazine, Australia, a regular contributor to James Halliday's *Wine Companion*, and the wine writer for *The Melbourne Review*. Her wine blog, newrubypress.com, was nominated for Best New Wine Blog at the 2011 Wine Blog Awards, and 'The Invention of Wine' won Best Editorial Wine Writing at the Born Digital Wine Awards, London 2012.

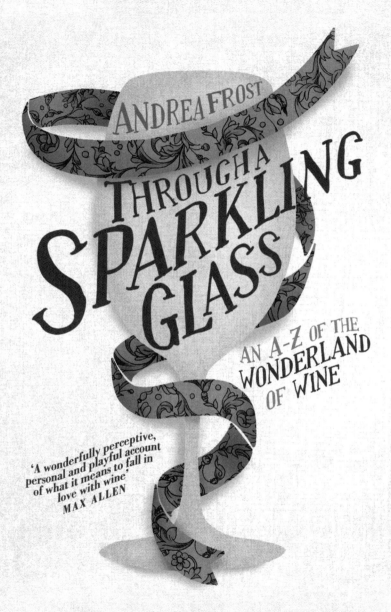

ANDREA FROST

THROUGH A
SPARKLING
GLASS

AN A-Z OF THE
WONDERLAND
OF WINE

'A wonderfully perceptive,
personal and playful account
of what it means to fall in
love with wine'
MAX ALLEN

hardie grant books
MELBOURNE · LONDON

Published in 2013 by Hardie Grant Books

Hardie Grant Books (Australia)
Ground Floor, Building 1
658 Church Street
Richmond, Victoria 3121
www.hardiegrant.com.au

Hardie Grant Books (UK)
Dudley House, North Suite
34–35 Southampton Street
London WC2E 7HF
www.hardiegrant.co.uk

Cataloguing in publication data available from the National Library of Australia.

Through a Sparkling Glass: An A–Z of the Wonderland of Wine

ISBN 9781742705316

Cover design by Josh Durham / Design by Committee
Text design by Peter Daniel
Typeset in Baskerville 10/17pt

Printed and bound in China by C&C

*To the wonder of wine*

# FOREWORD

## The invention of wine

God was sitting on one side of the boardroom table with his back against the window. A man walked in and introduced himself as Kevin from the Innovation Department.

'Very well, let's get on with this. I still need to hear presentations from several other departments,' said God, who'd been listening to pitches on how best to allocate his resources when he launched Earth in a few months' time. 'So,' he said, looking down at his notes, 'your idea is something called "wine"? Righto Kev, let's hear it.' He leaned back into his chair, but not before grabbing a couple of mints from the bowl in the middle of the boardroom table.

'Wine,' Kevin nervously read aloud, 'a drink made by a process called "fermentation", when broken grapes mix with natural yeast—'

'Hang on. *Natural* yeast?' God interrupted. 'What other kind would there be?'

'Good point,' said Kevin, scribbling notes on his sheet. He continued, still quite nervous. 'When this fermentation happens, it produces a liquid called "wine" that tastes delicious, makes you feel pleasure, has lots of flavour, makes you laugh and makes you think.'

'Laugh and pleasure and delicious?' said God, staring out the window. 'Sounds like more trouble than the bloody apple. Is it addictive?'

'Yes,' said Kevin, 'but only if you drink too much too often.'

'You run that past legal?'

'They said it was a grey area, sir. They suggested you might be able to cover it off in the commandments or the sins?'

'Oh come on, I can't make the Deadly Sins a dumping ground for everything that seems a little controversial. I've already assigned six of them,' he said, turning back to Kevin. 'How many can you have?'

'Seven?' suggested Kevin, shrugging his shoulders up to his ears.

'Still sounds like it could be a problem,' said God, not sold but intrigued by the idea of this drink made from grapes. 'Anyway, go on. So a liquid drink. Didn't I just approve something similar?'

'Sort of, that was water. Pretty neutral tasting and I understand you're going to make it in abundance, falling from the skies as it were. It will be different to my idea, because water will be so ubiquitous that people won't consider it precious and will pay scant attention to it.'

'Yes, well I'm still not sure if I've done the numbers on that one right … I think I might be short, but time will tell.'

'Ok, so wine is a different drink,' said Kevin, warming up and keen to get back to his idea. 'Not just any drink but a drink that is delicious, made from grapes, that makes you feel good and makes you wonder.'

'All that in one drink? It's sure gonna make this thing popular. I guess you want an abundant supply, too?'

'Quite the contrary.'

God looked confused. Kevin continued.

'This is where the concept gets genius, because it *won't* be abundant. We'll put limitations on it. Wine can only be made from certain grapes – and only once a year, and only in certain parts of the world.'

God sighed. It had been a long couple of days, and trying to understand these new product proposals was tiring him out.

'Well, how will I allocate land? I mean, there's a lot of competition. I can't make it all good for grape-growing. I'm starting to run out of space. There's the areas I need to allocate to the wildlife and keep open for their migratory paths, the very important wetlands, the plains of Africa, the rainforests in the Amazon, the oceans … they're the crucial things, and I've still got to put people on Earth. It's going to get crowded down there.'

'Yes, I have considered that. I thought maybe we could turn a negative into a positive. What I am proposing is that you make only certain parts of the world good for making wine, in fact, make some slices of land indescribably perfect for it …'

'Go on,' said God, intrigued.

'Save everything you have just for these special plots; program them to get the right part per million of the exact soils, the perfect amount of lean on a slope, just the right breaths of wind at just the right times, teamed with the right amount of rays of sunlight and the perfect warmth to grow ...'

God nodded slowly. Kevin continued.

'... the wine that comes from these places will be so exquisite that people will say it's been touched by the hand of ... I don't know, something magical.'

'Hmm, well if this land is so rare, how can people tell *where* to make wine?' asked God.

'Ok, you're gonna love this,' said Kevin, raising his hand as if to slap his own thigh at the thought of it. 'They won't know! Not until they have planted it there and waited a few years, sometimes even decades.'

'But ... but they could be guessing forever,' said God, starting to smile. 'I mean, people might plant these grapes in ridiculous places ... Oh you're a tease Kev, that's bordering on cruel,' he said, stifling a giggle.

'Think about it. This is a long-term vision. If you make it easy and everywhere, it'll be over in no time.'

'I see your point,' said God, more serious now. 'But eventually people will work out where these special places are, especially if there are so few of them. I mean, I'm not making them that stupid.'

'You might be surprised, sir.'

'Oh I don't know, Kevin ...'

'Ok, so here's another one. Not only is the land hard to find, and finite, but the quality of the wine changes with every single vintage because of the weather.'

'How will the seasons vary each year?' asked God.

'... *hello?*'

'Yes, of course. Weather, in the hands of the gods, isn't it?'

'I believe so.'

'Ok,' said God, back in the game, 'so what aspects can I change every single vintage?'

'You name it. Every single thing you do to the temperature, moisture, sun, wind, hail, frost will affect the wine. There will be so much to play with you'll have them on their knees.'

'Already assigned that.'

'Sorry, I didn't realise.'

'No problem. Well, how will the wine change? Give me an example.'

'Smells. Wine won't just have smells, it will have a perfume. A perfume made up of beguiling and complex aromas that draw from flowers and fruit, woods and herbs. And these aromas will change over time – they'll shift in just a few seconds and continue to do so over years. One day they taste like one thing, and the next it's like a fairy dropped by the cellar and mixed it up so it tastes a different kind of beautiful.'

'But it's just a drink, Kev, and it's quite confusing and always changing. Why will people want to drink it if it will be so complex?'

'*Because* it will be so complex. It'll be in their nature to try to make sense of things.'

'And as long I keep changing things ...' said God, trailing off into thought.

'... they'll keep trying to understand it,' finished Kevin.

God continued. 'I imagine those that are interested in it will be driven to talk a lot about wine ...'

'Oh God, you have no idea.'

'Could these wine people be a problem? I mean, a little too much?'

'No, it's fine. We've done research. None of the chitchat will fly outside of wine circles. Mostly, they'll keep to themselves. A little boring, but harmless in the main.'

'Well, a lot of this sounds a bit wishy-washy. What will they actually get out of it?' asked God, determined to make the idea a sensible one.

'It's kind of hard to put my finger on it,' said Kevin, 'but wine will be a drink that will join people together through its mystery and its allure. Entire countries will benefit from the wealth of wine, and communities and industries will be built around it. Social occasions will be made better because of it, and gastronomy will be better with it. It will be infused in every country's history, culture, tradition and place. It will be present at celebration and mourning, contemplation and revolution. It will be there for, and possibly be the cause of, the most memorable moments of people's lives.'

'I see now,' God said, smiling and gazing out the window. 'But what if they do understand it?'

'Give them a new vintage.'

'What if they manage that?'

'Create a new variety.'

'And if they get used to that?'

'Let them discover a new place to plant.'

'It's elusive, isn't it?' asked God.

'Yes,' said Kevin.

' … and beguiling …'

'Absolutely.'

'A nice idea, Kevin, but there are so many impracticalities, so many logical reasons why sensible people won't get into it,' said God. 'Remind me again: why will people keep going back to wine despite the madness?'

'Because we're also going to make it the most beautiful drink in the world.'

# CONTENTS

# PROLOGUE

Dad handed me a box of wines that I had stored in the cellar under the family home about twelve years ago and long since forgotten about. My first effort at cellaring, the collection was an enthusiastic mixed bag of wines that, I realise looking back now, I had assumed would make us all more interesting were I to put them away. There were some good wines, mostly quaffers beyond their time, but there was one gem: a Heathcote shiraz that, accidentally and to my delight, had aged beautifully over those twelve years. It was a graceful expression of strength that had silently been integrating and softening over all those years, even while I paid it no attention.

As my parents have aged, the cellar has become too difficult to access; it was really just a series of shelves built under the house and accessed by crawling through a door cut into the house bricks. As our family expanded, a deck was built out from the house, which meant you had to crawl under the deck before you could reach the door. There were injuries as Dad and I hit our heads or scraped our backs on the beams that ran above us.

Inside, the cellar was maybe four feet high – so you had to crouch the whole time. The only light came from a fluorescent globe that took three terrifying flashes to come on: three moments in which I expected to see a murderer or a ghost. Until those blinks brought light it was as black as a cave, and the only noises were the muffled thuds and voices of family life above. The floor of the cellar was the earth the house had been built on, which over the years had become smooth and polished like marble and gave the space a smell of ancientness.

The cellar was initially built for storing the ginger beer that Dad and his friends made on the apron of the garage every summer. It was a lively production line of three men making their brew while listening to the cricket. One was a New Zealander, and the other a Scotsman with English leanings, which meant the commentary over the cricket was as fierce in front of that garage as it was on the pitches of the MCG or Lord's.

Some bottles made it, some didn't. Those that did were served ice cold, clinking with ice and topped off with a sprig of mint, guzzled by holidaying children through the heat of summer. It is one of the most refreshing summer drinks: a cloudy, gingery fizz that still slakes the fiercest of thirsts.

Other bottles weren't so lucky. Occasionally, as we lounged on the couches inside, the hum of the fan doubling-back on itself droning in the background, we would hear a muffled thud and crash as a bottle with ever-so-slightly inappropriate levels of yeast and sugar exploded. Mum would call out to him from the kitchen, and Dad would groan and head off to assess the damage.

Over the years, the bottles in the racks changed from ginger beer to wine. I remember trips to Rutherglen and tales of ports and muscats, standard fare for Australian wine drinkers in those years. I remember holding giant tobacco leaves from the farms of Italian immigrants in the King Valley and surrounds, farms that have long since been converted to vineyards of Italian varieties. I remember empty Chianti bottles called 'fiascoes' swinging from butcher's hooks alongside pots and pans, and I remember hearing of claret and Rhine riesling at a time in Australia's wine history when borrowing such names was still allowed.

Dad took on a kind of sommelier role in our household, which made sense: the kitchen was a stage controlled entirely by my mother, a place so vast (it had two large stoves, two sink areas, and copper pots and pans hung from the ceiling and stuck to the walls) that it felt like both the engine and the control room of our house.

Dad served more quietly on the side. He waited on us and guests with all the ritual of a graduate of the court of master sommeliers. Whenever he brought wine out, he acted as though he were pouring the most expensive and precious bottle in the world. He would approach, half-bent from the waist, with the bottle presented across his arm to show the label, just as he imagined a traditional French waiter would. This was an embarrassing mime to endure as a young adult, particularly when we had guests.

But despite our groans and urges for him to hurry, Dad would pour a dash of wine in the glass and await our approval before continuing to pour.

During my very early teens, Dad took a part-time job at a winery restaurant in the nearby wine region. I think we needed the money, but I also wonder if he just wanted to serve a more grateful audience and shine on his own stage. While on weekdays he would dress in his grey suit, pack his briefcase and go off to work in the bank, on Sundays he would dress in black pants and a crisp white shirt, shoes polished to a navy-grade sheen, and serve wines to winery guests and tourists. He always returned with stories that he delighted in, sometimes of customers' uncouthness, but usually of news about the place, the wines or the owners.

Today his wine collection is kept upstairs and he still enjoys the ritual of wine service. At Christmas he will take you to the table where he has lined up his humbly chosen wines, waiting for you to marvel at his collection and share in his joy. On other family occasions he hovers to the side, waiting to serve you. And just like before, whenever the wine comes out he treats every glass as if he is pouring from the most expensive and precious bottle in the world. And as if he is pouring it for the most important person in the world.

'There is communion of more than
our bodies when bread is broken
and wine drunk.'

—M.F.K. Fisher

## A GLASS OF WINE

There is a line in *The Adventures of Huckleberry Finn* where Huck says, 'Soon as it was night out we shoved; when we got her out to about the middle we let her alone, and let her float wherever the current wanted her to; then we lit the pipes, and dangled our legs in the water, and talked about all kinds of things.' There are other sensory and gastronomic moments that should be appreciated like the way Huck sees the smoking of a pipe: to have a cup of tea is as much about the break and a quiet moment of peace or conversation; fish and chips on the beach, a domestic adventure to fan the flames of your spirited side; and a beer at the pub equals loyalty, camaraderie and ritual. When I think about a glass of wine I don't think of it as a drink, but a small and precious event, usually transitioning me to another moment more cohesive to sensual pleasures – eating, socialising, nothing – than if I were not having it. Whether it's a small and happy event or a loud and convivial one, never is it *just* a glass of wine.

# A LESSON ON CORKED WINE

I'm strangely happy when I find people who don't know what corked wine is. Not because I can roll my eyes and bore them witless, but because it's refreshing to remember that most normal people enjoy wine with a healthy but basic level of knowledge. It's like finding a family who grew up without TV that reminds us how blissful ignorance can be.

Recently I was having lunch with three men from the fat-cat end of town who insisted that the wine at our table was corked because it had some cork in it. 'Actually, that's not quite right,' I tried.

'Yeah, that bit there means it's corked.'

'No, it doesn't.'

'Yes, look closely, see that bit,' one of them said, pointing to a speck of cork bobbing in the deep, dark, inky shiraz.

'No, that's *cork*, not *corked* wine.'

It went on until they remembered they were in a dining room, not a boardroom. Out of options, they asked, 'Well, what is corked wine?'

So I told them all about a little thing called TCA, the tiny compound that gets into corks and, when the corks are put into bottles of perfectly crafted wine, infuses the wine with a taint that ruins the winemaker's faultless work. I explained how TCA can be difficult to detect, especially in heavier red wines whose robustness can weather small amounts, but how it very easily upsets white wines, infusing them with the awful smell of mould in even minute amounts. Rather than realising the wine is corked, you might just think the wine is not much chop and never buy it again. I also explained the value of screwcaps on wine, and that many of the best producers in the world are now turning to them and have been for years ...

Oh, and I politely suggested that if they really were relying on the sound of a popping cork for romance, then they might want to invest in a few more tricks. Let's face it, the pop only lasts a second, and the work is often done by someone else.

A few nights later I opened a bottle of sancerre, an unopened leftover from a dinner party. Instead of finding the racy, leaner style of sauvignon blanc made in the region, I got wafts of mildew. It was corked. I put it aside and twisted the lid on a rosé instead. As I was enjoying the wine, a friend walked through the front door. Before I knew it, he had helped himself to the sancerre, taken a gulp, looked curiously at it, then at me and asked with importance and emphasis, '*What* am I drinking?'

## HOW TO TELL IF YOUR WINE IS CORKED

If your wine is corked it will smell mouldy or musty and, in heavily tainted wines, quite unattractive. The first thing to go in a tainted wine is the fruit or perfume, so a wine that is quite lifeless and dull might also be corked, even if it doesn't smell overtly mouldy or musty. If you are unsure, ask your waiter or sommelier – they should replace your wine with a fresh bottle. Twist-top closures, like what you'd find on a bottle of olive oil or balsamic vinegar, are used as an alternative to cork to eliminate cork taint. They are widely used in Australia and New Zealand, and to some extent in America – but less so in Europe, where tradition rules.

So I started to tell him all about a little thing called TCA ...

'I LOVE it!'

Oh.

'Where's it from?' he asked, looking at his glass from underneath as if the answer might be written there.

'Well it's from a region in France ... but um, it's also ...'

'Awesome, that's what it is.'

A curious position indeed.

I could have continued, explaining it was corked and not good, but who am I to tell a man that he's not enjoying himself when he evidently is? Surely one of the points of wine is its subjectiveness? What I think is a good drink may be someone else's vinous nightmare, but that shouldn't undermine my pleasure. Anyway, it's not like I poured it for him.

I know, I know, I can see the other side of the argument sitting earnestly on my shoulder, wagging its finger and shaking its head, asking about my responsibility and duty to inform. How is anyone supposed to learn if no-one guides them?

My friend continued, 'This wine is just gorgeous, I'm trying to think what it tastes like …'

I poured him another glass and let him hang in his bubble a while longer.

'Bliss?' I suggested.

## A LOVELY CUVÉE

E veryone seems to know their favourite style of champagne. It wasn't until – and because – I was nearing my trip to Champagne that someone asked me to declare mine.

'I don't know,' I said.

'But you must have a favourite.'

I said again that I didn't.

'Come on, your favourite style, what is it?'

It's terrible, this adult version of peer pressure. I was tempted to blurt out a big name – I mean, I did go to the Mumm tent at the Grand Prix once and I totally loved that. But I stuck to the truth: 'No, I really don't have one.'

'Oooh, controversial.'

Really?

I wasn't trying to be; but I did begin to wonder how it was that I got to this point in life having achieved so many other things, yet failed to know my favourite champagne style. Was this serious? So when I got to Champagne without any champagne preferences, I was determined to develop some.

'Each cuvée we make is a different person with its very own different character.'

I was with a fifth-generation Champenoise. (The Champenoise like to anthropomorphise their wines. I found it both charming and helpful.) Using the cuvée-as-a-character idea, we focused on three wines – the traditional champagne, the champagne blanc de blancs and the champagne blanc de noirs.

'This person is a good balance of the terroir,' she said of the first, the traditional champagne, made from pinot noir and chardonnay. 'It is not a slick guy from the city, nor a farmer from the vines, but a good balance of both.'

I know this guy, I thought. Solid, family man, gentrified farmer,

## A ROSÉ BY ANY OTHER WAY

There are two ways to make champagne in a rosé style. 'Rosé d'assemblage' is to add a tiny amount of red wine — like adding a dash of red cordial to water to get a pink drink — to the white wine before continuing on with the normal champagne-making process. This typically makes a lighter style rosé champagne. Champagne is the only region in France that allows rosé to be made in this way. The other way, known as 'rosé de saignée' is where red grapes are crushed, the juice left to extract only a small amount of colour from the skins (the longer the contact the stronger the colour extracted) before being bled off and used to make champagne.

knows how to fix a fence and decant a wine. Sure, I get this. I took another sip. I liked him, but he was never going to be my favourite.

Next up was the blanc de blancs champagne, made from 100 per cent chardonnay grapes. 'This is a female,' she said, lifting her nose from the flute. 'Yes, definitely a feminine character with lots of finesse and elegance.'

Why yes, this champagne *did* taste feminine. All light and lovely, with wafts of white flowers and honey, a lick of minerality and a long and lovely length. Finesse and elegance: I could do that. Maybe I was a blanc de blancs girl. Perhaps I could do favourites after all. Besides, this was a delightful wine.

Finally, we tasted the blanc de noirs grand cru, the wine made with 100 per cent pinot noir grapes, the variety which gives the champagne fullness, richness, strength and power. 'This is the tough guy, the powerful guy, but he is not just one-dimensional, not like a football player who is only about strength. He is strong, but he can also move. A dancer.'

Well, yes, I thought, noting the fuller pinot noir aromas and the rich and opulent palate — the power. As I tasted I noticed something else, something more fluid, attractive. Without thinking I said, 'It's still a very elegant style.'

'Yes! You see? The dancer.'

I was all over this.

She went a step further, saying she could also use her intimate knowledge of the cuvées to pick wine for guests, even those she didn't know. A sort of oenological character profiling.

'We can tell just by looking at people what sort of cuvée they will be,' she said. 'If we have a worker with dust on his boots—'

Before she could finish, I said, 'The traditional.'

'Trés bien.'

I was so with her. I couldn't wait to hear what she thought my new favourite wine, the blanc de blancs, said about me.

'This,' she said, giggling, pointing to the blanc de blancs, 'this we always know to pour for the girl who turns up with the big blonde hair, the high heels and lots of make-up.'

Oh.

Like I said, who needs favourites anyway?

❧ TASTING NOTES ❧

❧ There are three grape varieties that can be used to make champagne, two of which are red. These are chardonnay, pinot noir and pinot meunier.

❧ Blanc de blancs: This 'white of whites' is champagne made from chardonnay only. Because of this, blanc de blancs are typically finer and more delicate − perfect aperitif wines.

❧ Blanc de noirs: 'White of blacks', this refers to champagne made only from pinot noir, pinot meunier or a blend of the two grapes, making a fuller style of champagne.

Adding a strawberry to a glass of champagne is about as complementary as throwing a pink dye bomb into the Trevi Fountain. It is not meant to be. If you are after aromas of strawberry, or the nod to romance you think it represents, order rosé champagne and knock 'em dead with some early Sadé.

## A MINERALITŸ LESSON

It was a breakthrough moment – not only for its simplicity, but because it was one of those times when you finally understand the series of small and surprising events, some of which must have seemed quite unfortunate at the time, that helped to make something so wonderful.

I was in Champagne learning about the sequence of natural events that make champagne taste as it does.

We had driven up and parked on a hill above the village of Villers-Marmery, with a clear view across the valley floor. Behind us was the Montagne de Reims, the mountain range that gives its name to the mostly pinot noir–growing region of Champagne. The lush forest that rides the spine of the range is a cluster of beech, oak and walnut trees that is home to deer, boar, foxes and rabbits. The forest is also home to bunkers and bloodshed from the human wars that came before. It was early October, and the treetops were turning from lush dark greens to deep rusts and ember reds, like a stovetop element slowly heating up before our eyes. Underfoot, between the rows of vines, licks of white chalk peppered the uneven ground.

'There are five things that make up terroir,' I was told, my guide looking at my notebook, waiting for me to write before he handed them over. I obeyed. 'Soil, subsoil, altitude, exposure and gradient. Change one, you change the terroir.'

With nature as his classroom and a combination of figures drawn in the ground, fistfuls of crumbling dirt and arm-sweeping gestures to the hills and valleys as his teaching materials, my guide explained how Champagne – the place – works.

He explained that an inland sea covered the area 70 million years ago. When it dried up 20 million years later, it left behind the crushed remains of the belemnite crustaceans that had flourished in the sea. He said that, when compressed, the shellfish remains formed a layer of chalk a few hundred metres below a covering of topsoil. Twenty million years ago, an earthquake shook the land so ferociously that it broke up the chalky seabed and pushed it up above ground, like the steps of an escalator rising out of the flat, still with the layer of soil on top. Another earthquake 10 million years later pushed the hills we were standing on even higher, filling in the gaps between the steps with slopes of white chalk. This explains why – when you look at Champagne now

## A MINERAL CONTROVERSY

Minerality and similar terms have been used to describe wines such as champagne and chablis for some decades. Recently the term has been used with more regularity throughout the wine-tasting world, and this has caused some controversy. The issue up for contention is whether or not you can taste mineral notes from stones or minerals in the ground that have been extracted by the vines and, ultimately, have made it into your glass of wine. This has caused all sorts of discussion, but when you think about it, it makes more sense that we might taste minerals than banana, pineapple, coffee, matchsticks and gunflint.

– the forests are on the top in the layer of fertile soil, the vineyards are on the slopes where the chalk is and the crops remain in the fertile flatlands that yawn across the valley floors of Champagne.

Nothing but vines can grow in this harsh chalk. And not just any vines: all of the best grand cru vineyards grow on this type of belemnite chalk. Vines, of course, need poor conditions to be the best they can. They respond well to a kind of viticultural tough love. When it rains, the chalk draws the water away from the surface and stores it deep in porous layers that act like water tanks for the drier times.

Brilliantly, the chalk also retains the warmth of the sun's rays and throws it back up to the vines, helping them nudge the 11.5 degrees they need to ripen. This is vital in a climate as marginal for viticulture as Champagne.

The scene before me was clicking into place.

My guide went on. All the villages, he explained, are built low in the valleys, where the potentially harmful fog collects, and the vines are planted high on the rises.

'That's dedicated of them,' I mused, trying to imagine if anyone building a house these days would make such a sacrifice.

'Yes,' he said, 'but without the grapes there is no wealth.'

He continued explaining that it is these old crustacean deposits, rich in limestone, that help develop the acidity in the wines – something as vital to champagne as the bubbles themselves.

Then he explained something I always hear thrown about when it comes to champagne. It completed the picture perfectly.

'To lick,' he said, crumbling a handful of earth, 'this chalk tastes of nothing.'

'And to drink?' I asked.

Minerality.

# AGEING

The wine was presented at dinner with as much ceremony as if it were a new child. Its arrival was announced to the guests while it was carried in two hands, as though its preciousness were fragile enough to crush. It was placed in the centre of the table and adored. As I admired my hosts' generosity in the offering of a very old wine, I got to thinking about how readily we accept ageing as a notion of superiority in wine – yet not in ourselves.

Few would disagree that we live in a youth-obsessed society. The virtues of remaining forever young are sprawled over billboards and flaunted in TV ads, conveyed in movies and sprinkled through magazines. If we're not having the message shoved through the windows to our souls, we're being promised eternal youth in lotions and creams, lasers and lipo, plugs and tucks.

It's not just appearing young that we are fixated on; the pressure to succeed is being felt younger and younger. Career selection starts at an age when we are yet to know *ourselves*, let alone what area of the world we wish to specialise in. As Gloria Steinem said recently, 'Our generation thought life was over when we were thirty; your generation thinks you have to be successful by then.'

Frankly, I am not sure about this obsession with youth. I never know what I would say to a younger version of me – there seems so much to address, and I can't think of anything worse than being a younger version of myself again.

As they promised all those years ago, life gets more complex with age – but it is also better. There are so many more things to believe in, passions to stand for and deeper satisfactions to be had.

Only possible, of course, with experience and age.

As I sat with my friends and looked lovingly at this very old wine, I couldn't help but wonder if we could learn a thing or two about ageing in life from ageing in wine.

Take the vines. It is almost universally accepted that older vines make better wines. Young vines have vigour and brightness on their side, but it's the older vines that are the most sought after to make the best wines. As vines age, they produce a delightful complexity and intensity in their fruit. How lovely to think that extra years on vines are prized and nurtured, celebrated and rewarded.

It's even better news for vines from the best vineyards. Not until a vine is between ten and fifteen years old is its fruit deemed mature enough to go into grand cru wines. Winemakers acknowledge that the younger vines lack a certain ... something.

We also tolerate the slowing effects of age in vines more than we do in ourselves. Late last year I was in Alsace, wandering the vineyards of an exquisite domaine in Turckheim on the charming Alsatian wine route. We took a turn over the hill to one very old vineyard. As we stood amongst its rows, I noted how lovingly the ninety-year-old vineyard was spoken of. High on the hill, overlooking the medieval towns on the valley floor, backed by the Vosges mountain range and with the Black Forest of Germany in the distance, the vines could not have had a more beautiful place to grow. The canopy of the vines was thinning on top and their trunks were thickened and twisted at the base – telltale signs of older vines. But here, these gnarled old trunks were considered a thing of beauty. The vines still produced fruit of exquisite quality – there was just less of it, and it took a little longer to grow.

In viticulture, time is allowed for character to express itself. In an industry that has been making wine for thousands of years, it is expected that fifteen to twenty vintages will pass before a vineyard will start to show its magic. Some winegrowers claim regional expertise only after inheriting hundreds of years of local knowledge. Can you imagine being allowed forty, fifty or sixty years to hit your straps? They say late bloomers are rare not because talent in older people is rare, but because talents that might develop when we're older often don't get the chance to shine. They lie buried beneath an earlier chosen career, a restricted identity or the lack of freedom to explore. Many die with the music still in them.

Perhaps the most obvious sign of our respect for the ageing process is in the cellaring of the wine itself. How much reverence we have for a cellar full of ageing wine, and what efforts we make to enable this ageing to happen. A very particular set of environmental conditions is cultivated to help the wines age – cellars must be dark and still, with the right humidity, a constant and perfect temperature, away from excessive light or constant vibration. Unlike what we're fed in today's media channels, it's not about trying to hold on to the wine's youthful qualities, but about developing and celebrating its aged ones. The end game here *is* age: to develop, to change, to become more complex.

As I raised my glass and saluted the very old wine, I realised that in many respects we get it right with our attitudes to wine. It's not about trying to be what we once were, but becoming what we can be.

## ❧ TASTING NOTES ❧

❧ The ageing process is relied upon to click all the parts of a
wine into place, to make it more seamless and complex. Tannins
and acid will soften, oak will integrate and fruit-forward characters
will tone down. This ageing process happens when small amounts
of oxygen come into contact with the wine over time.

❧ Ageing will not improve bad wine and for a wine to age well,
it must be capable of ageing, and made to do so.

❧ Older wine is not always better, just different. Much
wine today is designed to be drunk quite soon upon release,
minimising the need — though not the desire, should you wish —
to age most wine.

## ALBARIÑO

O n my way home from a talk, I ducked into a bar to find one
seat that, because it was alone, no one wanted. I relished it
for just that reason. I enjoy, from time to time, eating out on my
own as a nice break from the familiar. I have also come to believe
that if you can enjoy a glass of wine out, alone, you'll be fine for life.

The brown-haired girl was drinking wine but not drunk, and
unaware of her loudness, especially as she raised her voice to be
heard above the increasing noise of the crowd.

'I mean, we've got to remind ourselves that we're in a pretty
unique time in our lives right now. Look at us; here we are, out
and about at one of Melbourne's cool little gems, having a few
wines and some tapas,' she said to her friend, who was looking

around at the crowded bar, as if to be sure.

They scanned the room from their seats at the floating bar. It was full, heaving even – some people were standing in the doorway and others were hanging out in the laneway outside, waiting to be signalled in.

The loud girl continued. 'You know, if you had a family you'd have to plan this stuff like, eight months ahead!' and, as if to celebrate her freedom, she raised her glass and enjoyed a full mouthful of white wine.

I guessed they were in their late twenties because of the theme they were talking about; I think every age group has a few themes that preoccupy them and callings they feel obliged to answer.

The two girls seemed to go a fair way back; they spoke of people from years ago. 'What ever happened to Amelia? I totally forgot she even existed!' and 'What about Sally? I feel like she totally checked out on me like years ago.'

They were single and, despite the loud girl's generous attempts at looking on the bright side for both of them, I don't think they wanted it that way.

'See?' she said as she heard about a friend's new boyfriend. 'She got proactive. It's a good lesson. Can we make a pact, to be a little more proactive?'

My tapas arrived – some oily fried peppers and grilled prawns in garlic – along with another glass of albariño, a white Spanish wine.

'You know,' went on the loud girl, 'If you want to you can. I know someone who went from single to getting married in a year. She decided this was her year, knew where the silver platter was, got proactive, got out there and found her love. Now? Blissfully married. Gorgeous.'

They drank to that.

### VINO BLANCO

Albariño is a Spanish white wine native to Spanish Galicia, but attracting interest in other parts of the winegrowing world. It's your go-to white for tapas. Well, one of them. Albariño's charm is that it has a lovely and generous nose sometimes of peach and apricot aromas woven with a delightful enlivening line of acid.

There was another story, about a family friend, not seen since university days. There was some talk, some events were recounted, and the climax to the story: a boyfriend. Which, for them, meant happily ever after.

'See? Proactive!'

The conversations and planning continued with gusto.

I wanted to tell them that it doesn't really matter: not everyone's happy having done those things. Some do, some don't, some are happy, some aren't, those that aren't will be again and those that are will have other seasons. But you never believe anyone who's not from your decade, especially a woman who would tell you she's happy sitting at a bar, on her own, eating tapas and drinking albariño, smiling to herself occasionally.

Later, the loud one came back from the bathroom and started talking even though she was still six feet from the bar and her friend was on her Blackberry. 'Oh my god, why didn't you tell me?' she said, laughing and sliding back onto her stool as her friend looked up from her phone. 'I had chocolate all over my face!' and they both burst into laughter, revelling in what was indeed a happy and unique time in their lives.

# ALSACE

I walked the cobblestone lane that ran the rampart of the medieval village, passing the restaurant twice before I stepped inside and away from the cooling autumnal night. It was closer than it looked on the map – I still hadn't scaled down and adjusted to the fact I was in a village, not a city – and I took the extra paces in the fresh air to wake up properly from a recent nap. Earlier that day I had drunk two tulip-shaped glasses of the local Alsatian riesling on the main cobblestone street, alone at an outdoor table as I watched the crowds pass.

The restaurant was called 'Pierrot le Fou', Peter the Crazy, because that was what they called him when he was building the restaurant – or so his mother-in-law told him.

I had read that it was intimate, only able to seat eight people in total at any one time, and that Pierrot le Fou was quite a character and would take the time to host you. I had dined on my own for over a week, something I had initially longed for – in fact, it was something I had come to do – but for the first time I welcomed the idea of being engaged with someone else. Even crazy would be fine.

'Bonjour,' I chimed in time with the bells on the door.

'Hello, Welcome,' came a woman's voice from behind the desk.

She showed me to one of the three empty tables in a room the size of a billiard table, and, before she disappeared, indicated that Pierrot was coming.

And then he appeared. Maybe it was the medieval surrounds, the turrets and the cobblestones, the half timber houses and the stone walls, or the introduction Pierrot was given in the brochure left in my apartment that made me anticipate someone equally as themed – but when he arrived, he was not that at all.

Pierrot le Fou looked like a cross between Ernest Hemingway and Santa Claus, his eyes round and kind and soft. He wore canvas pants held up with braces that reached around his rotund tummy, which was all wrapped up with a long black apron. He had a white beard and head of hair and round-framed glasses that hung on a chain around his neck.

'Enchanté! You are staying at Jean-Paul's. We welcome all his guests with a cocktail,' he said excitedly, in English but with a very French accent. He returned to the kitchen and came back with a tall glass of wine. Inside it had a twist of orange peel, one of the local grey gewürztraminer grapes bobbing inside, some mint and a lick of sugar around the rim. It felt like a small and special gift, and I was grateful for it.

Pierrot left me to enjoy my drink. The décor of the room showed a full and happy life the owners were proud of. Shiny enamel art was on the walls, and the room was dotted with team sport photos of a younger Pierrot, cooking certificates and qualifications, wooden carvings and vases filled with flowers.

After some time, Pierrot came out with two menus. Handing me one, he sat opposite me at my table, the smallest of the three available. 'We go through it together,' he said as he placed his glasses on his nose. He read out each dish from the menu in detail, describing every cut, ingredient, preparation and style of cooking, watching me to make sure I understood, sometimes pointing to his arms and legs when he needed the word for 'thigh' or 'tail' or 'wing'. He read so carefully and slowly it was like watching him read his part in a play for the first time.

Pierrot came to one dish and said it was for two, but that he would read it anyway. It was goose neck, sliced down the middle, stuffed with goose fat, apple and sauerkraut gratin. 'But I cannot make that for one. What will I do with the other half of the neck?' It's ok, I said, I understood.

I chose the sardines in truffle butter and seasoning for entrée and the lobster tail with ravioli parcels for main. 'A nice dinner,' he said, approving, and got busy preparing my order. To go with my dishes, we decided on a half-bottle of vouvray – he thought it was a little drier and that it would help with the oils.

I was quietly disappointed with myself that I hadn't ordered something local from the grand cru vineyards that rose up from this walled village and whose wines I had tasted all day, but I was eager to please my host and took his recommendation.

He poured my wine and left to prepare my meal. As I brought the glass to my lips I noticed it had across the front an etching of a couple having sex. She was sitting upright, one arm propped against a wall, her legs wrapped around his body; he lay diagonally across her, his back and naked buttocks toward me, his face on her outstretched arm, one arm hidden from view, perhaps on her lower back, the other arm holding her bent leg up to create space for his body between her legs.

I asked him about the glass as he delivered my sardines. 'Yes, you can buy them in a set of six,' he said, as if that were my query.

'All like this?' I asked, pointing to the twisted figures now lying on a bed of vouvray, wondering if it was ok to smile.

'No, there are six different pictures but all doing, ah ... you know,' and he walked off, laughing with the confidence of a man who'd had his share and now had the fun of using it for decoration.

With the cooking done, Pierrot came out to check on me as I was eating my main. I asked him to join me by stretching my arm out to the seat opposite and offered him a glass of wine. He accepted, sat down, poured, held up his glass and nodded. We discussed topics that were easily shared between well-meaning strangers. About rugby: 'Wherever there is a sport, there is an Australian.' The Tour de France: 'Evans is a very elegant man.' Fencing: 'It's like dancing, you must be fast and have good legs.' At this he jiggled his upper body, trying to show me how fast fast was. About Americans, whom he always welcomed: 'They were kind to me when I lived there as an artist and they helped us in the war.' We spoke of Riquewihr, the medieval town we were in, how beautiful it was and how lucky it was to have survived the wars. I mentioned how our towns at home are not so old.

We spoke of Champagne, where I had spent the previous week, and how it was not so lucky in the wars. Pierrot had not been there for twenty years but had many fond memories, many of which came to him as he smiled at the empty space in the air in front of him: 'Bollinger is a beautiful wine,' and 'Pol Ro-jay rosé has the finest bubbles.' 'Dom Perignon, oh, the shape of the bottle and when the sabre comes out,' he struck his arm away from his body, removing the top of an imaginary bottle in an old-fashioned and traditionally ceremonious manner of sabrage. 'And Mumm, it has the softest bubbles,' he trailed off, smiling as he visited an old and pleasing place. 'It's like a gift from God.'

If I ever slowed the pace of my eating because I was talking, he waved his open hands at my food to make sure I didn't stop. 'Eat.'

Pierrot asked me for a favour: to send him a postcard of the platypus and the Tasmanian devil. 'I love the platypus, with its bill. It's so fast and clever. And the Tasmanian devil. Well it's like me, bad every day,' he smiled. 'But they are sick,' he said, stroking his jaw as if it were he who had the cancer. 'They must look after them.' I nodded, as if I knew exactly who to take the message to.

He fiddled with the corner of the business card I had given him when I told him why I was there, 'to do with wine', which of course was close to the truth.

'Isn't this beautiful?' he said, smiling. 'One hour ago we didn't know each other existed, now we are talking like we are old school friends.' We touched our glasses and drank the last of the vouvray.

### ABOUT THE REGION

Alsace is the French wine region on the border of Germany that has in fact been German at various points in its history. Those who have travelled more say it's one of the prettiest wine regions in the world, and I can attest to its beauty — a charming wine route that runs along the spine of the Vosges Mountains, with medieval towns tucked into the folds of a mountain range dotted with old castles and ruins. As a wine region, it's most famous for white wines, including pinot gris, gewürztraminer, riesling and pinot blanc.

As we parted he reminded me about my promise of the postcards. 'To receive such things like that gives me another dimension in my life.' I was already wondering how I would find them, and how it is that we fail to keep such promises.

At the end, replete, I again thanked him very much for his food and for his company. 'It's my job,' he said, waving the compliment away. 'Humans can't stay apart for long, they need to be engaged, otherwise it is not life, it is no fun.' Perhaps remembering I was there on my own, he added, 'Not for long anyway.'

As I swung my bag over my shoulder and left the restaurant, stepping back onto the cobblestone laneway that was now shiny with the mist that had crept over the walled city, I thought that this man – who was called crazy, who cooked me dinner and became my friend for the night, and who said that people weren't meant to be apart for too long – was not so crazy after all.

# APERITIFS

These lighter-in-style alcoholic drinks served at the beginning of the night have quite a job to do, not least because they actually fulfil several roles. Of course, there is the traditional expectation that these usually dry drinks, mostly white wines and cocktails, are used to stimulate the appetite and get you ready for the meal ahead. Let them do this, and be sure to eat when they do – it's not cheating, it's exactly what is supposed to happen!

But the aperitif is often the most crucial drink of the evening for many other, less obvious reasons. I recently watched a friend offer aperitifs to his dinner guests. One after the other he asked what they'd like, and one after the other it became evident that these drinks had a much more important role to play than merely preparing guests' palates for the meal ahead. There was one serve of drinks, a beer and a white wine, that acted as the facilitator between a couple still feuding from the drive to the dinner party; another that relieved the day's tension for a corporate man under mounting pressure; a glass of prosecco broke the ice for friends who hadn't spoken since That Time. And, really, anything alcoholic can be used as a truth serum by the old-timers to interrogate the newcomers.

When selecting appropriate wines for aperitifs, look for dry, unwooded or sparkling ones, and while you're pouring, see if you can notice what else, aside from appetites, starts to fire.

## ❧ TASTING NOTES ❧

THESE WINES FUNCTION BEAUTIFULLY AS APERITIFS:

❧ Champagne: With searing acidity, precise lines, spirited bubbles and a refreshing and cleansing palate, champagne is the benchmark for all pre-dinner wines.

❧ Prosecco: The sparkling wine heralds from the Veneto region in Italy, but is loved the world over. Nothing complex about it, prosecco is dry, bubbly, often less expensive than champagne and, in some circles, a little bit cooler. Should be consumed as young and, as the Italians might say, as often as possible.

❧ Riesling: German or Australian, French or New Zealand – a chilled glass of riesling that comes naturally with lots of refreshing and enlivening acidity will get everything in order for dinner.

❧ Txakoli: From the Basque Country in Spain, txakoli (pronounced 'char-koli') ticks all the boxes for an ideal aperitif – it's super dry, brimming with acidity, lower in alcohol and has a little bit of show. Pour it from arm height to bring out the slight spritz in the wine.

## AUTHENTIC WINE HAPPINESS

There are many rituals and techniques around the world that have evolved to make you focus on the good things in life, rather than the bad. Of course, like exercise and eating well, an attitude of gratitude is something that's easy to abandon, but feels nice when we don't.

What would it be like if this appreciation was applied to wine tasting? After all, at formal levels of analysis, the intense scrutiny often seems to focus on the negative rather than the positive. One of the things that we are taught when we first learn about wine tasting and connoisseurship is to look for the faults. We are taught that there is *probably* some shortfall or inadequacy that stops the wine from being a gold medal or trophy winner, or perfect or great or worth it, so let's scrutinise for it.

We look at the liquid and hold it to the light as if through an invisible magnifying glass, looking for fault by sight detection. We swirl it with the intention of amplifying the aromas, good and bad, and we taste and aerate and swallow to look not just for the good but most certainly for the inadequacies.

Well, absolutely, there *might* be something wrong with it; nature is neither consistent nor perfect, so when made at the hand of man – an even less perfect specimen – why would one of nature's most beautiful expressions be so?

But what would happen if we were to look for the good in wines? Would it change our perception, not just of the wine, but also of the tastings themselves, by removing some of the anxiety that comes with wine tasting for many? According to proponents of the exercise, it might even reach out of the tastings and make our whole disposition a little brighter.

The next time you taste a wine, rather than start with the various techniques of scrutiny, look for what is good in the wine and list that. Don't limit it to a formal tasting technique or box-ticking, but take it as wide and far as your brain can go.

For example, I had a beautiful cool-climate Australian syrah the other night. Instead of a tasting note, I might say that I was appreciative to nature for being able to produce something alcoholic from grapes (still gets me from time to time) and appreciative that someone had the sense or luck to plant grapes on that

## THE GOOD LIFE

About a decade or so ago, Dr Martin Seligman spawned a movement and wrote a book called *Authentic Happiness*. The movement came out of the idea that psychology had spent half a century focusing on illness and, as a result, had undermined the importance of those things that Aristotle, as quoted by Seligman, called 'the good life'. The goal of the subsequent positive psychology movement is 'to find and nurture genius and talent' and 'to make normal life more fulfilling'.

site, because if they did it an acre away, it might not taste as good, and if it were someone else, the land might be devoted to grazing sheep instead. I also admired those winemakers who continued to experiment with new styles, as they did just a few vintages earlier, with this one; and I was also grateful for how stunning it was, because the company I was keeping were, in turn, very happy with the wine.

This is not to undermine the truly great wines, nor forgive truly terrible ones – they will elevate or demote themselves accordingly. But why not enhance things that are already good, especially if it's in pursuit of 'the good life'?

Just as focusing on the good in life can help bring about the good life, so too can focusing on the good in your glass of wine. Sure it might have *something* wrong with it, but we all do – and in wine, as in life, it shouldn't be all that you see.

'There are two ways to live: you can live as if nothing is a miracle; you can live as if everything is a miracle.'

—Albert Einstein

## BAD VINTAGES

B ad things do happen to good people and bad conditions do happen to good vineyards, devastating the vintage and destroying crops through no fault, rhyme or reason.

THREATS TO
THE SUCCESS OF
VINTAGE

Certain vintages can produce poor wines for any number of reasons that nature dishes up. It might be that it's too cold, preventing the winegrowers from ripening their fruit properly; it might be too hot,

Hail, rain and disease, or a lack of sunshine, or too much of the same, are the great enemies of vintage. Other than that, it's easy.

making it difficult to retain good acid levels in the grapes; or things might be going along wonderfully until rain, hail or disease changes everything. The lovely thing about wine – well, nature, really – is that no matter how bad the vintage, there will always be another; it's the way of life and always has been.

*'Life is not meant to be easy, my child but take courage: it can be delightful.'*

—*George Bernard Shaw*

# BIODYNAMICS

G rowing up, I lived near a Rudolf Steiner school and used to hang with kids who went there. Kids who went to the Steiner school were wild and earthy compared to my world of school uniforms and 'God Save the Queen' assemblies. The Steiner kids weren't afraid to strum a guitar in public, were frightfully expressive in contrast with my other friends, wore socks and sandals at the same time and carried macramé-handled school bags which, so the whispers went, didn't carry any school books because at Steiner school you just sang songs, called the teachers by their first names, and only started your tutelage when you felt good and ready. Unreal! To me, these kids might as well have gone to school in Disneyland and had Mickey Mouse as their teacher. Which is funny, because my dad thought the same thing.

Rudolf Steiner (1861–1925), the Austrian philosopher responsible for this good-and-ready schooling system, was also responsible for the school of biodynamic agriculture: a method that approaches the farm as a self-sustaining and interlinked universe that relies on the relationship between animal, mineral, vegetable and the cosmological. It also dictates that you farm according to the cycle of the moon and use certain preparations mixed in cow horns and buried underground – which is where traditional farmers get nervous and the industry starts to divide. But as one biodynamic winemaker said to me recently, 'I don't know if I believe in the process, but I believe in the end result.'

The 'for' side supports biodynamic viticulture because it is less harmful to the Earth and is synergistic with nature, producing wines that have more flavour and express the place they are from and are not unnatural concoctions whose links to the region are blended away beyond recognition. What's more, it looks after the land for the next generation.

Arguments against biodynamic viticulture, aside from calling it witchcraft and poppycock, are that it makes difficult vintages unmanageable, and wines inconsistent and unstable. Whatever your stance, people becoming conscious of what they do to the Earth can only ever be a good thing.

## BLENDS

B lends and wine blending, though different, both have the aim of making a more complex, measured and consistent wine.

On one hand, winemakers blend different varieties together to make a more interesting wine; many believe few varieties are interesting enough on their own. It's a bit like saying, 'I like that you wear all black – it's slick, stylish, flattering, striking. But why don't we add a lick of colour with a red scarf, just to make the overall look more interesting?'

What's more, some varieties, even the magnificent ones, have little weaknesses – Achilles heels, as it were. Cabernet sauvignon is said to have a donut: a hole in the middle of the palate that is often filled up by adding a little merlot, like a plump squirt of jam in the middle. Shiraz is often made silkier with a tiny addition of viognier, taking a savoury wine and making it more aromatic and slipperier to drink.

### ALL ABOUT BLENDING

Most wines are blends, even if the additions are in amounts that don't require acknowledgement on the labels. Famous blends include champagne, Bordeaux, Châteauneuf-du-Pape and Penfolds Grange. Popular varietal combinations include cabernet merlot, semillon sauvignon blanc, grenache shiraz mouvedré and shiraz viognier.

The varieties are usually listed on the label in the order of the highest percentage in the blend. Sometimes this percentage is declared, other times it's not; many countries allow an addition of something else — up to 15 per cent — without declaring it, to allow winemakers to make up for vintage variation.

The other instance of blending is when winemakers blend different *batches* of the same vintage and variety. For example, a chardonnay might be made with some batches that have been aged in new French oak, some in old, or some with lees stirring and some without.

Some famous wines are made as blends because it's not always possible to get consistency: Bordeaux, so close to the sea, can get humid, so relying on single vineyards can be risky. Champagne is so cold it often struggles to ripen the fruit, so winemakers need to mix it with other varieties and vintages to create a consistent and drinkable style.

The point of blends and blending is to take the good bits, recognise the weaknesses or seasonal variations and add something else to make a wine that is greater than the sum of its parts.

Just like teamwork. It reminds me of a time at business school, a place big on teaching you about teams – how to manage one, how to look good in one, how to align with key players, how to behave so you don't get pegged as the renegade that everyone hangs out to dry.

We undertook an exercise where groups were given the same scenario (we were in a plane that crash-landed in a desert, no-one knew where we were) and a list of things (matches, flares, water, salt, stuff like that). The task was to choose eight of the fifteen items to take with you. Naturally if you got this wrong you might get a low mark or die – the most horrifying options possible to MBA students, in that order. You do this individually and as a team. A high-functioning team will get a higher score than the individual – the theory being the sum of experience is greater than its individual parts. But this only applies if, and only if, you work well together.

One team included a dominant type-A alpha male and a quiet female international student. Throughout the exercise the quiet woman tried to have her say, but every time she spoke, she was railroaded by alpha dog who, based on personal judgements, assumed she knew little about the subject. At the end, the team scored much lower than the quiet female student, who got a perfect individual score. Turns out she was a former SAS SWAT Marine Navy SEAL in a covert and secret international army or something clever like that.

That's the trick with blending, as with team building: you've got to know all about your component pieces and how much to add of each. If not, the end result might be far worse than the individual thing you started with.

## LIGHTWEIGHTS

If you've noticed some traditional-shaped bottles looking slightly skinnier, you're right. Some environmentally conscious producers are turning to lighter weight bottles for all the right reasons.

# BOTTLES AND BOXES

## BOTTLE SHAPES

Probably the first evidence of wine marketing is the distinct bottle shapes that various regions adopted as their own. Bottle shapes were adopted by different wine-producing regions at first for quite practical reasons – durability of transport – and then eventually to create differentiation and distinction. Today, many regions still use them to identify their wines, and some, such as Alsace and its use of the tall and elegant wine flute, are required by law to do so. When there are no laws stipulating bottle shape, a wine typical of one region that is made in another region, such as cabernet sauvignon made in Margaret River, is often bottled in the traditional bottle – in this case the Bordeaux bottle – to give a nod to the style.

The most common shapes are the champagne, Bordeaux, burgundy and German/Alsatian wine bottle shapes. The Bordeaux bottle's tall, high shoulders are to catch the sediment, of which there is more because of the nature of tannic varieties, while the burgundy bottle features sloping shoulders and a smaller punt.

Today many old-world regions, including those mentioned before, require by law that these bottle shapes are the only ones used to bottle wines from those regions, while in other countries, variations in colour, shape and glass weight abound.

## BOTTLE SIZES

Does size matter? Yes and no. Larger bottles such as jeroboams and magnums are sought-after collector's items, as they age the wine more slowly. Smaller bottles are said to speed up the ageing process because the amount of surface area in contact with air is greater, percentage wise, than in a large bottle. But what of the standard size, and how did we come to settle upon the 750-millilitre size for our wine bottles?

I like to think that, some time around 1518, there lived in Rome a man who worked in his family's business. It was built at the top of a very long hill. This man was strong and big and fit, and he performed the jobs in the business that involved strength and muscle rather than contemplation and intellect. One of his most important jobs was to cart the toddler-sized amphorae of wine — those large, tall clay jugs that had been used to make, serve and store wine for the past century or so — to Friday-night drinks for his twenty-eight family members.

One day, when he was in the village collecting the first of many of the night's amphorae, he noted some men making vases for the tourists from glass. He had the brilliant idea of making glass bottles to carry and serve wine in, rather than lugging the massive amphorae around.

At first he had the idea that the bottle should be only a little smaller than the amphora that he was carrying. He asked the men making the vases if he could try it and they generously obliged, offering him a stool and his own glass to blow for a share of some of the wine.

However, when he sat down to blow the glass into shape, no matter how hard he tried, he could not blow a bottle larger than around 750 millilitres. He tried and tried but every time he did, the new glass wine bottles came out that size. Well, over the coming years he made hundreds. Everyone loved the convenience of this single-serve wine bottle and today we accept it as the standard size.

### 🍇 TASTING NOTES 🍇

🍇 It is thought that the standard 750-millilitre bottle of wine is related to the lung capacity of glass blowers in the 16<sup>th</sup> century.

🍇 As well as the standard size of 750 mls, there is also the magnum (1.5 litres, equivalent to two standard bottles), the jeroboam (3 or 4.5 litres, equivalent to four or six standard bottles), and, upwards several shapes and sizes, the nebuchadnezzar (15 litres, or twenty standard bottles), right back to the problem that the glass-blower was trying to solve.

### CASK WINE

I can remember summer barbeques from my youth, when the entire neighbourhood descended on each other's above-ground swimming pools. We children spent the day in a pool, only sliding out like wet hungry seals for a sausage in bread and to watch highlights of the cricket as we waited the requisite thirty minutes before diving back in. Men smoked cigars and pipes and drank glasses of claret while the ladies sipped Rhine riesling.

I learned these foreign words from the cardboard boxes they came in, right before we tore them apart and ripped out the empty silver bladders. We wrapped our grubby little mouths around them and filled them with air, cringing if any remnants of wine touched our lips, or if any stale grapey air puffed in our faces like the breathy kiss of an aunt right before she got in the car and drove everyone home. And there we had our very own pool toys. How times have changed.

Truth is, the invention of the wine cask did more for the increase in awareness and consumption of table wine in Australia than anything else. Table wine boomed through the 70s thanks to the cask or, as it was fondly mocked, Château Cardboard. Prior to this, Australians were largely drinking sweet fortified wine. This invention, that made savoury table wine available at the squeeze of a nozzle, coincided with Australia's opening up, through post-war immigration, to other cultures' food and drinks. At one point, cask wine was responsible for more than 50 per cent of wine sales by volume, today it is slightly less. You know who you are.

### WINE IN A BOX

The first cask was introduced in Australia in 1965, but the concept took off in the 70s.

The advantage of a cask is that, as the wine doesn't come into contact with any air, there is no oxidation — a process that typically starts the minute a wine bottle is opened. Casks are wildly convenient; you have up to a month to drink the wine once it's opened, which saves on wastage if you're the kind that I have heard about who doesn't drink it all at once.

## BUBBLES

To make the best quality champagne possible there is a particular, expensive and rather laborious way of infusing bubbles into the wine. But I wonder what is gained from knowing

## THE MAGIC OF BUBBLES

Oh, all right – but just a simple explanation, and only of the original technique of making bubbles in wine, known as the Traditional method. (There are two other lesser quality and less expensive methods.)

Bubbles in champagne come about because of a secondary fermentation that happens in the bottle. When fermentation occurs in still wines, carbon dioxide is one of the by-products. But when it happens in a bottle with a very tight cap on, the gas is dissolved back into the wine in the form of bubbles. This initially happened accidentally and was once considered to be quite a problem; now it happens when the winemakers add a kind of liqueur to the blended base wine, setting off the secondary fermentation.

There is a lovely story that Dom Pérignon, when he first discovered bubbles in his wine, said 'Come quickly, I think I am drinking stars.'

how bubbles get into champagne – or any other sparkling wine for that matter.

Before you read about it, think about what you may or may not find – it's even possible such knowledge might detract from the product in question's beauty. But I do know there is pleasure to be gained by just accepting and delighting that the bubbles are there; I am certain that if you focus on that for a moment, your champagne will be even more pleasing to drink. It's like you're holding your very own fireworks show, a stream of fine and excited bubbles twirling their way to the top before bouncing on the wine's surface. Lovely, isn't it? You know, you don't always need to peek behind the curtain. Sometimes, it's just nice to believe in magic.

## CARRYING CAPACITY

When I first started reading about wine it was easy to remember where vines grew. There were two fat bands: one at the top and one at the bottom of the Earth, between about 30 and 50 degrees of latitude on either side of the equator, within which vines could grow. Champagne was the most marginal climate at the top, and pretty much no wine grew in the middle. It all ended with New Zealand and Chile, the most marginal wine-producing climates in the south.

But these days it's not so straightforward – the bands are more like ECGs from a heart attack than straight lines. Due to technology, new wine drinkers and changing markets, wine is also now made in Thailand, Vietnam, Indonesia and India, and in England – further north than Champagne. Go back only two hundred years – as quick as a hiccup, considering wine has been made for seven thousand years – and the expansion is even more telling.

Wine, like everything managed by humans, including our population, has been expanding at an increasingly rapid pace.

But when we expand, something else shrinks. It has to. Earth has a carrying capacity – it's already set and it's not negotiable.

Around the globe we are starting to see shortages of farmland, and some wealthy countries are already leasing land from others.

Some scientists have even imagined taking food production off the farm and into custom-built buildings known as 'vertical farms' in major cities.

Even when it comes to something as lovely as vineyards, we're starting to bump into ourselves. In McLaren Vale, South Australia, vineyards and suburbs are running into each other as development caters for swelling populations. In Germany, plans are underway to construct a car bridge that traverses the Mosel Valley, slicing through some of the world's best riesling vineyards.

This problem will not go away; it's predicted that by the middle of the century there will be two billion *more* people on earth, taking us to nine billion. Many countries – including the most developed – already live beyond their means.

It is easy for us to feel that, because we are using land to make something as precious as wine, we are exempt from such issues: stick it to the agro-chemical, genetically modified corporate-owned monsters instead. But I fear that is unintentional denial. We are also involved, as humans, as farmers, as population growers, as consumers of nature's resources, no matter how much we admire it first or how lovely our end product. Are we any different because we are making something that has aesthetic properties and that provides pleasure? I don't think so; nature doesn't know the difference.

I don't know what this means we should do – I really don't. Others who know more say there is plenty to do: slow our population growth to limit the amount of space we continue to take over, treat the land we have developed well, stop wasting resources, slow our consumption, take a long-term view and, most importantly, protect the wilderness and living creatures that cannot protect

themselves. 'As the most intelligent species on the planet,' says
David Attenborough, 'this is our moral obligation.'

But what I am sure of is that we can start by being aware and
very, very grateful – because if one thing is for certain, we won't
fight for something if we don't care for it, and we won't care for
something if we don't notice it.

'The care of the Earth is our most ancient and
most worthy and, after all, our most pleasing
responsibility.'

—*Wendell Berry*

## CELEBRATING YOUR OWN TERROIR

There is a very particular set of things, as complex as a galaxy
and more secret than the thoughts of the dead, that makes
us individually and exclusively who we are. It's a unique combination of genetics, nature and nurture, experience, wisdom and
everything else that makes each one of us un-replicable anywhere
else in the world.

Just as there is a set of things that make you uniquely you,

## A SENSE OF PLACE

'Terroir' is a French term, though the essence of its meaning is now being embraced by winemakers outside of France. It refers to the unique combination of natural things that make wines from a certain place taste as they do. For these qualities to be expressed, it requires winemakers to stand aside and allow the grapes and place to shine.

there is a lovely and magical term in the world of wine that refers to the set of things that make wine from a certain plot unable to be replicated anywhere else in the world. 'Terroir' is the unique and combined effects of the soil, sun, rain, weather and other things particular to that plot. It's like a sprinkling of nature's fairy dust that casts a 'spell of place' over sections of vineyard the world over.

The effect of this means that pinot noir grapes grown in one block make a wine that tastes different to wine made from pinot noir grapes grown an acre – even just a row – further along the road. It's this vineyard personality that many winemakers aim to express in their wines.

But a vineyard's personality, just like a person's, can only be expressed if it is allowed to. In wine, it is done by minimising human intervention in the vineyards and wineries. Letting what is, be.

Reasons for viticultural personalities are wildly different the world over. In some places, eucalyptus trees impart distinctive mint characters into the wines; in Heathcote, the oldest soils in the world contribute to the wine's character. Many maritime regions are tempered by the moderating effects of nearby oceans. In Chablis, slate and mineral characters are a feature of the wines, and many Italian whites are infused with a distinct and lovely salty character.

In individual plots, differences become more specific until tastes are detectable but the reasons unexplainable. Ask a French winemaker what it is you can taste and they will shrug their shoulders and say, 'It is just the terroir.' Ask someone why they are like they are, they might say the same thing: 'It's just who I am.'

And just as there are so many wines that celebrate their own sense of place, so too should you celebrate that unique and magical set of things that make you as un-replicable as any of the very best wines in the world.

## CELLAR-DOOR TASTING

It was someone else's idea to visit a cellar door before lunch on a recent weekend away with friends. Nice, I thought. Maybe my friends, more wine civilians than connoisseurs, were finally getting involved. I had the chuff of a country-club parent whose child finally asked for an argyle vest and a nomination to the golf club.

The staff set us up for a tasting – the glass, the list, the aromatic-to-heavy spiel. I looked around and noted my friends grabbing

## TIPS FOR CELLAR-DOOR TASTING

Cellar doors are a wonderful way to try wines and wine tasting in a friendly and often gently tutored environment. Most cellar-door staff will have a process to manage you through. Let them guide you; it's a nice way to wander and ask as many questions as you want. Taste in order of light wines through to heavy ones; start with lighter white aromatics through to richer white wines, then rosés, lighter red wines, heavier reds and finally fortified wines. Depending on where you are, you might need to make an appointment, so call ahead. Nominate or organise a driver early on and be prepared — you might need to pay a small fee to taste wines at some cellar doors. Buy a bottle and take it home; you'll have much to discuss at the dinner table when you share it with friends. This is how wine conversations start.

their glasses and listening. Finally, it was happening. I began to daydream of the wine club we would start.

The wines were poured and the woman began. 'This is our sauvignon blanc, which is made in a lighter style.'

Two girlfriends had their glasses filled with the light, bright and aromatic wine, sipped it, nodded, then moved to a corner of the room and started chatting as women do on a Friday night at a bar in town. I swear, at one point they looked to the rest of the group, wondering who was going to get the next round.

Another friend asked to start on the reds. 'Big ones,' he said. Finding one he liked, he declared it to be delicious.

'Would you like to try another one of the same variety but from a different vineyard?' asked the woman behind the counter.

'No thanks,' he said, holding out his empty glass, 'I'll stick to that one.' He looked around at me proudly. '*What?*' he said. 'I like it.'

Ah, who could blame them?

To the civilian, the transaction that goes on at cellar doors can often be quite uncomfortable. It's a place where something fun crashes into something formal. To enter a room full of strangers, with a line-up of wines, a bucket of someone else's spit, some tasting notes and a price list, can be enough to drive even the most enthusiastic away. A shame really, as this little room offers a remarkable opportunity to frolic in a new wine experience like ducklings in a pond.

Tasting at a cellar door is quite often your first experience with wine tasting – not drinking, but *tasting* – and if you're not used to the conventions, it can make you feel as though you'll be mocked at your first dribbled spit, wrong descriptor or clumsy pronunciation. It's even more confusing when you compare it to the 'arms wide open' appeal of every other alcoholic drink. Buckets, spittoons, swirls, colours, notes, lists and verticals – no wonder wine tastings get a bad rap from the kids.

Looking at my lovely bunch of friends, I noted the gap between what was on offer and what they thought was on offer. If they were interested, I might have told them some basics. But then, so what if they didn't follow the list from light to dark, so what if they didn't spit anything? All these rules and conventions about what you should and shouldn't do at the cellar door! It's enough to make you drink. Which, come to think of it, is the whole point.

## 'Be yourself; everybody else is already taken.'

—*Oscar Wilde*

# CHAMPAGNE

For many years I was of the belief that putting on a façade was as great a sin as telling a lie. But in the fullness of time, and with the richness of experience, I have come to learn that sometimes, putting on a brighter face is simply showing the world that you have a greater capacity for life than it does for dishing out hardship. I think everyone has a mask. Freud certainly thought so. Most people I know have something they smile in spite of and, as I was driving away from Champagne, I wondered if it was possible for a place to have one too.

Synonymous with celebration, glamour and wealth, champagne is the wine as comfortable lounging across double-page spreads in fashion magazines as it is at premier events the world over, enabling those who aspire to such glamour a taste of the good life – sip by sip, glass by luxury glass.

So naturally, when I arrived in the region, I was expecting a buzz of red carpets and gowns, heels and gloss, song and dance. But champagne the image and Champagne the place seemed so vastly different that I wondered how one was born from the other.

The first thing I noticed was that Champagne seemed bleak: a landscape of rolling hills and wide, yawning valleys with little that was natural and recognisably 'champagne'. Her natural icons are intangible. They are her stories. They are her myths. They are as much about the exotic places she has travelled to, the parties she has been to and the people she knows than anything she has to show at home.

History doesn't properly explain her international reputation for luxury and celebration either. There were the French kings, nearly all of whom were crowned at the local Reims Cathedral, thereby making Champagne a centre of celebration. But those festivities stopped two centuries ago, and what came after that was not so joyous.

At the crossroads of important trade routes, Champagne was contested for centuries – as far back as Attila the Hun, and as recently as the last world war. The only other feature as ordered as the rows of vines in Champagne are the rows of crosses erected in honour of those who fell across her land.

Beyond the luxury houses, the architecture also belies the opulent image. Instead of domes that strobe with gold like those in nearby Paris, some buildings in Épernay still bear the scars of bullets. In many villages the closed architecture, defined by

## A DRINK FOR CELEBRATIONS

Champagne's propensity to offer a happy disposition has ensured it remains present at celebrations and important moments – personal and seminal – throughout history. Champagne was present at the signing of the Maastricht Treaty and has been toasted at a long line of royal marriages; it has launched some of the most famous ships in history, including the ill-fated *Titanic*, and has been drunk on the summit of Everest and to celebrate successful space missions. Winston Churchill requested only to drink bottles of 1945 Pol Roger until his death. I guess, for good reason, he was fond of that year.

inward-facing buildings and high walls, was initially designed to protect a community tired of being invaded so often, over so many years. Flower boxes of happy geraniums attached to the walls are an attempt, I was told, to appear more welcoming to the modern and curious world.

These layers of hardship and sadness that lie beneath the image she presents to the world seem even more tragic because of champagne's propensity to offer a joyous face for other people's celebrations. Her bright disposition has been borrowed, time and again, to lift a melancholy mood in others.

Beautiful, glamorous, perfect champagne – with such a history? And yet still it is poured.

I'm reminded of family dynasties that continue to perform in the spotlight, despite being laden with their own tragedies.

I thought about why Champagne, whose history is bleak and scarred and fought over, cultivated an image that is the complete opposite. But then I figured it was precisely because Champagne has a history that is bleak and scarred and fought over that it chose this image.

'Birds sing after a storm,' said Rose F. Kennedy, 'why shouldn't people feel as free to delight in whatever remains to them?'

And delight they do. The large and magnificent Champagne houses continue to lift the velvet rope for visitors wishing to spend some time between the sheets of luxury; emerging growers make their own wines that speak of their place and of their land; biodynamic producers are turning back the clock on viticultural progress, ridding their blocks of chemical advances and showing a new and greater sensitivity for the land. Even the vines show resilience to adversity, being the only things able to grow in such difficult conditions.

All of them are in their own way continuing to make a wine that is as beautiful to drink as it is to taste, as pleasing to bestow as it is to receive, and as credible a drink as any to lead a celebration.

Champagne was a place I thought I knew, but after seeing beyond the façade I realised I had misjudged her. She is, after all, just like any of us. As I drove away I thought that, despite our scars, we could all learn something from Champagne's great capacity for life and revel in the delights that remain ours.

## CHAMPAGNE CORK REMOVAL

I REMEMBER WATCHING THE NEWS AS A CHILD, AND HEARING MY DAD MUTTER, 'HEATHENS!' WHENEVER A SPORTSMAN STOOD ON A PODIUM, SHAKING A MAGNUM OF CHAMPAGNE AND SPRAYING ITS ENTIRE CONTENTS OVER THE GRINNING GRID GIRLS. I USED TO THINK HE WAS A SPOILSPORT; NOW I UNDERSTAND.

When removing the cork from a champagne bottle, the aim is for a gentle pfff, a sigh, a small whisper; not a podium-style volcanic eruption. The cork should emerge without losing a single drop of the precious liquid. To do this, follow these steps:

1. Remove the foil that covers the cork and its metal cage on the top of the bottle.

2. Twist and remove the metal cage, keeping a thumb on the cork and the bottle pointed away from you.

3. Now hold the bottle at the base in one hand, and the cork in the other. Twist the bottle — not the cork — slowly and gently.

4. As it loosens, hold on to the cork to prevent the escaping pressure from shooting the cork sky high. Wait for the sigh, remove the cork, and enjoy your bubbles.

*'Remember gentlemen, it's not just France we are
fighting for, it's Champagne!'*

— *Winston Churchill*

## CHANGE

I t is necessary for humans to believe that the most advanced
and current information available is also the most appropriate.
I suspect this makes us feel we are the most advanced version of
mankind that ever was and, even more importantly, that we had
something to do with it.

It's confronting to think that we are counterproductive to

civilisation or nature or some other large and mysterious system. Not on our watch!

Confronting as it might be, world history is littered with beliefs that were commonly held to be true at the time, only to face obsolescence or redundancy in future generations or after the acquisition of new knowledge. The passage of time does not guarantee a process of linear improvement on any level – it never has.

The things we believe about gods, nature, religion, medicine, law, expansion, war, sexuality, feminism, beauty, marriage, environment, good and evil have all been modified along the way. If you like change, you can be sure it's coming.

Wine is not exempt.

One of wine's charms is that it changes over time. It is suspected that this trait elevated wine's importance throughout history; without any scientific explanation, this drink made from grapes had a seemingly magical way of evolving during its life.

We have often celebrated our beliefs, only to update them, sometimes quite significantly, down the track. Ladies lounge, anyone? Right now, there are probably ideas we believe to be correct that will evolve, at best, or be deemed inappropriate, or even erroneous, at worst.

Yes, even on our watch.

*'Everything changes and nothing remains still ... No man ever steps in the same river twice.'*

—Heraclitus

# CHARDONNAY

I t was four against one. I was trapped again.

'Shall we just get a bottle to share?'

'Sounds good,' they sang, distracted by the buzz of a group get-together. The camera was already out, heads gathered around. There was a wedding to recap, an after-party to debrief, and notes to compare on who was there and who went where.

'What about a chardonnay?' Knowing my audience, it was more of a dare than a request.

As sure as night follows day, it started: 'It's too oaky', 'It's too creamy', 'It's daggy', 'It's not sauvignon blanc', 'I can handle it unwooded', 'I prefer pinot gris ... don't I?'

I love chardonnay, so I get it a lot.

'It's not that you shouldn't drink chardonnay, it's that you shouldn't drink *bad* chardonnay.' I was competing with wedding gossip. I didn't stand a chance.

Things have changed a lot with chardonnay since Australians made it as big and full as they once wore their shoulder pads and Benatar hair. It was, as the parents say, all the rage. It got us noticed. It made people love us. And then it made people blame us for making bad chardonnay. Hence the attitude.

Chardonnay's only fault is its flexibility and willingness to dance to any winemaking song. See, chardonnay is one wine you can do a lot of things to. In fact, it's one wine that benefits from work from the winemaker. Like a pair of jeans, they can stay classic or you can give them an acid wash, fade them, darken them, slash them, roll them or make them stretch. Some styles are more enduring than others and some may never see the light of day again. Chardonnay is a bit like that; there's a lot you can do to it and a lot that was done.

Though Australia was very good at bringing a new style of chardonnay to the world wine stage, many countries contributed to the ubiquity of chardonnay in the 90s. It was planted in most wine-growing regions that allowed it.

They planted it because of its viticultural congeniality, but also because it's the white grape that makes one of the most revered white wines in the world.

Cutting chardonnay from your wine repertoire is like culling a classic white shirt from your wardrobe, or burying old denim. Chardonnay is not optional, but essential, versatile, beautiful and highly desirable. Chardonnay can be drunk with more foods than most white wines and comes in so many versions that you'll never get bored – from the lean and minerally styles made in cool-climate regions to the more layered, fuller bodied styles whose complexity arrives at the hand of a few more winemaking tricks.

Saying you don't like chardonnay because of what you tasted in the 80s is like saying you don't like fashion because of what you wore in the 90s.

'Some of the best wines in the world are chardonnay.'

'Sorry, did you say something?'

'No, it's fine,' I said. 'Anything left in that bottle?'

STAY GOLD

Chardonnay produces a spectrum of flavours and layers and levels of appeal that make it hard not to fall for. From austere and minerally chablis to the chubbier, more complex Burgundies, to the range made in California and Australia, great chardonnays are like a complex, creamy, cosy waft of loveliness. Chardonnay can be grown anywhere wine is made and welcomes a few introductions from the winemakers, such as oak, adding to the possibilities and complexity of the wine. This availability, as well as its versatility with food, makes it a safe white wine to order and a wonderful white wine to drink.

## COMPANY

For me, one of the most important but least discussed factors when it comes to enjoying wine is company. Whom you deem to be good company to enjoy wine with is as personal as your view on the afterlife, but the wrong company can put a bad taste in your mouth and ruin your favourite wine.

For my choice, good company must include good conversation. More elusive than the perfect wine, a good conversationalist is a unique mix of listening and talking, flattery and authenticity, that seems increasingly hard to find. Too much talking and you do all the drinking, not enough and it becomes hard work.

In this case you might choose your own company over bad company, and this is fine too. Important even. It's a fading virtue to be able to take pleasure in your own company: if you don't like your own company, don't expect anyone else to.

Finally, when considering who you're with, consider your wine *as* company. A good wine will be more than a drink. A good wine will engage you, make you conscious of it, entertain you and take you places.

*'An intelligent man is sometimes forced to be drunk to spend time with his fools.'*

—Ernest Hemingway

# CONNOISSEURSHIP

A certain question has perplexed me for many years: is wine connoisseurship a good or a bad thing? Few could deny that there are many barriers to participation in wine and I have often wondered: if you could start the industry over, would you invent it like this again? I mean, would you make wine connoisseurship the path to wine appreciation?

As I have run blindly head-on into an understanding of wine, the dichotomy presented by connoisseurship has often confused me. If it *is* a drink that anyone can and should access, why do we taste it in such an inaccessible way? If wine is just a social thing to be enjoyed among friends, why not just enjoy it among friends? And if we fall in love with it for reasons of intimacy and humanity, why do we talk about it with scores and numbers?

Many will argue that the tastings and tutelage are necessary because wine is such a complex subject; that we need these systems to navigate our way through the detail. But as certain as I am of the detail, I'm not entirely convinced it came like this: is wine detailed because nature made it that way or because we did?

Besides, the world is full of detail. You could also approach the topic of fashion in a similar way; it too has origins, history, culture, thread, weave, pedigree, provenance, craftsmanship and economics. I mean, we could, but we don't. Wine doesn't own detail.

Maybe it's just that the system of judgement and assessment is so entrenched in the culture of wine that it's an association that's hard to shake. Occasionally, new voices join in to try to loosen things up, make things cool and simplify wine's complexities in an effort to provide an alternative to the formalities of connoisseurship. But, really, I have often wondered if valiant efforts by wine connoisseurs to simplify the topic are not really trying to change what is. Rather, they're impassioned attempts to bring others along with them for the ride.

Another oddity that makes the question hard to answer is that, in a world that is getting less formal – sociologists have long observed that traditional rituals have gone from the Western world – why hasn't the ritual of wine connoisseurship faded to something more relaxed? Why do more people than ever continue to flock to the formalities of wine connoisseurship when formality is so passé?

It's not like it's something taught in schools that we blindly continue in adult life. It's not something that is essential to daily lives, nor is it hard to avoid, like mass-produced consumables. Wine connoisseurship must be sought out. And it is.

I suspect we might pursue wine via connoisseurship for reasons not entirely evident to us. Are group tastings an answer to some human need to come together – a community in a wilderness where events as elaborate as a coronation or as casual as a drop-in are fading? For some, perhaps the ritual itself is what they're attracted to.

The analysis of wine also encourages us to do something philosophers thought essential to human happiness: conscious reflection. In those moments of reflecting on something attractive, wine, in many ways, keeps us more alert and conscious of the universe; in an increasingly materialistic world, it's an important perspective to have, whether we know where it comes from or not.

But as beneficial and admirable as these elements are, I think they are enabling steps bringing us closer to the real reasons for wine connoisseurship, which is a process of aesthetics, the search for and appreciation of beauty.

Perhaps this is wine's real trick: that wine connoisseurship is not about wine at all, but 'the science of the beautiful', as Oscar Wilde said about aesthetics.

*'It is, to speak more exactly, the search after the secret of life.'*

—*Oscar Wilde*

## DECANTING

One of the great ceremonies of wine service, decanting has two purposes. The first is to separate the sediment that collects at the bottom of old wines. The sediment comes from compounds derived from seeds, stems and skins that over time collect at the bottom of the bottle. This is less common these days, given the improvements in winemaking and the fact that not that many people age wine that long. The other reason is to aerate and soften younger wines that might need to let off a bit of steam to be more approachable.

### ❦ TASTING NOTES ❦

DECANTING OR AERATING YOUNGER OR MORE ROBUST AND COMPLEX WINES CAN BE DONE IN ANY NUMBER OF MODERN DECANTERS; THE ACTION OF POURING THE WINE OVER AS MUCH SURFACE AREA AS POSSIBLE SOFTENS THE WINE, HENCE THE ELABORATE TWISTS AND TURNS SOME DECANTERS HAVE.

Opening a bottle to let it breathe for an hour or so before meals doesn't do very much, as so little of the wine is exposed to air.

Decanting an older wine is slightly more complex. Keep in mind the aim is to separate the sediment from the liquid:

🍇  Stand the bottle upright for 24 to 48 hours before you plan
on serving it.

🍇  Open the bottle with care; it's old, remember.

🍇  As you pour the wine into the decanter hold a light to the
bottle near the shoulder or neck of the bottle so you can see
when the sediment moves near the opening.

🍇  When the sediment starts to tip down the neck of the bottle,
slow down, then stop before it gets to the opening so it does not
go into the rest of the wine in the decanter.

## DETAIL

I f you think about the trajectory of wine education, formal
or otherwise, it is mostly about the accumulation of details.
I guess this is the basis of all education – start with some letters,
then form words, sentences, stories, ideas and analysis.

Wine is not really so different; we start by learning many and
varied bits of information and equipping ourselves to seek out

these details, usually starting with the sample to hand. When it comes to the variety, we scrutinise for details of clone selection or traits that express typicity of variety; we look for signs of the region, of the vineyard or soil type; we look for the minutiae of the winemaking choices, such as types of yeast or the use or type, toast or age, of oak. We look for tannins, green or hard, rough or velvety. We even look for intangible things such as a sense of place or the winemaking philosophy.

It's quite a ride to zoom in so tight and takes enormous skill – to see the masters at work in such a task is always impressive.

What's more, that this much detail can exist in a bottle of wine continues to astonish and bewitch and allure people – wooing them to the wonders of wine.

But sometimes I find, with wine or life, that the closer we get, the less we seem to see. And because of this it can be helpful, from time to time, to take a step back.

Try it. The next time you are looking into a glass of wine, scanning and scoping for detail, acknowledge and note it, then step back and send your gaze through your glass, and perhaps into the room. Look around at your fellow tasters and their reactions, then maybe beyond to the window, to the city and bars and all the people enjoying and loving the wine they're drinking, the food they're eating, and the conversations they're having. Then take it up and out, to the vineyards where the wine came from, and then the country, the region, the world. As you're zooming out, you'll also be able to see other things, non-wine things – family, history, cities and countries.

Then, eventually, you'll find yourself floating around in the deep blue sky of space.

Looking into a glass of wine and searching for detail, there's only so much you can see, but there's an awful lot you can view from space. I think it's called perspective.

*'Go further than you planned.* **Ask for the moon:** *you will be surprised how often you get it.'*

—*Paulo Coelho*

## Dionysus

I n Greek mythology Dionysus was an important god, a direct descendant of Zeus, father of the gods. Dionysus represented the bounty and mystery of wine. Dionysus's story was also used to communicate the downsides of excessive wine consumption. Dionysus was later adopted by the Romans and adapted into a simpler version known as Bacchus.

The Dionysia was the series of festivals held in honour of the Greek god of wine, Dionysus. The most famous was Anthesteria, celebrated in the spring in Athens to mark the maturing and opening of the previous year's vintage. A three-day-long festival, it was an all-in affair from country to city when festivals and celebrations occurred. Slaves were set free to join in the celebrations, animals were sacrificed, bread, fruit and water were offered, elaborate processions proceeded and tragedies were performed in theatre. Generally, a celebration worthy of a wine god: a tradition I think we should consider again.

The Cult of Dionysus was eventually celebrated by the Romans in a less official way: all-night parties, probably orgies – known as bacchanalia – eventually sullied the reputation of the god of wine. This, along with the expansion of other religions, saw the events, celebrations and cult banned.

## ENJOYING WINE

I t is one of wine's anomalies that for centuries people have revelled in its heady pleasures, yet we still insist on mainly recording its technical aspects – as if these were more important than the resulting pleasure from the drink itself. It's the pleasurable effect of wine that drove its initial expansion, from its accidental invention in Georgia some seven thousand years ago, and it's the thing that most of us look for when choosing wine today.

Yet still, all the talk.

I concede that some of it is important, and much of it is interesting. I mean, what is information but context to amplify and add interest to your subject? But if it's pleasure we really drink wine for, then, just as a guide to life appreciation should

### HOW TO ENJOY WINE

For those who would like to pursue the enjoyment of wine rather than just the technical aspects, consider the following factors: companions, setting, food, music and your state of mind.

be more than a lesson in biology, a guide to wine appreciation should be more than a lesson in vinology.

So what do you need to enjoy wine?

Well, I came up with my own list but it's hard to know if it's the things on the list that make wine enjoyable, or if it's the wine itself that makes these items more pleasurable. I suspect it's a bit of both, and to partake in the things on this list is not just about enjoying wine, but enjoying life – which for me, anyway, usually go hand in hand.

# ETIQUETTE

M ost people I know who make a point of highlighting the importance they place on etiquette and manners can be kind of rude. I know of people who would cheat on a spouse, but be outraged that anyone might cheat in tennis; who write thank-you letters for an event where they spent the night insulting the host; who ask how you are, but don't listen to the answer; who won't splay a knife and fork on the table, yet will answer their phone there; and who would never talk with something in their mouth, unless it was a mouthful of someone else's business.

Perhaps P.J. O'Rourke was right when he said, 'Manners are a combination of intelligence, education, taste and style mixed together so that you don't need any of those things.'

Wine is rife with rules and conventions, particularly at wine tastings. But these steps were designed to ensure you get the most from your tasting without interfering with the process for anyone else. When you first attend a tasting, it can be intimidating. At my first tasting I had little idea what I was in for. My view back then was that I had just been given twenty wines for free. Had it existed then, I might have Facebooked this fact for my friends. The woman sitting next to me looked at me as I happily sipped, then drank my wines.

I can't be sure, but I imagine my notes read progressively something like this:

'Yum.'

'Nice.'

'Lovely.'

'Whoa.'

'Is this still mine?'

'Am I getting tested on this?'

'I forget.'

'Can I order yum cha on this mat?'

The woman next to me asked, 'Is this your first tasting?' with a knowing smile.

As complicated as the rules may seem, don't be intimidated by the wine-tasting etiquette; it's there as a guide and will help you understand the wines. It's also brilliant at making you look terribly busy and distracted if the host asks you what you think of the wines and you don't know what to say.

But most importantly, don't be intimidated by the performance of others, because I have come to believe that for many, manners are not offered to another to be polite, but to be more elitist – which I imagine is the exact reason some people attend wine tastings.

## ❦ TASTING NOTES ❦

❦ Swirling breaks the surface of the wine, thereby releasing the molecules and making it easier to smell the wine's offerings.

❦ Put your nose in the glass and smell the aromas.

❦ Take a sip and note what you taste. We are hardwired — for evolutionary reasons — to taste only bitter, sweet, salty, sour and umami.

❦ You might also sense the texture, tannins and a sense of the slcohol content of the wine. Wines that are high in alcohol often feel 'hot' to taste.

❦ Neurobiologust Gordon M. Shephard recently made a new and important step forward; he proposed that the most important smell inputs are those sent to our brain when we breathe *out* with a mouthful of wine (or food); and it is the combined and concurrent effect of taste (from the tongue) and smell (from the brain) that creates our perception of flavour,

❦ So, swirl the wine and note the aromas; sip the wine and note the taste; then breathe out with a moutful of wine and note the *flavour*.

## FAMILY TREES

Grape varieties, like people, are usually a cross between two different parents. Sometimes this is intentional, done in nurseries under careful conditions to create a variety with desired characteristics from each parent. Other times these crossings can be spontaneous, as such things often are when a pair is left alone in a vineyard.

Until recently a vine's parentage was mainly guesswork, but new DNA profiling techniques and the work of ampelographers (grape experts) have uncovered some surprising lineage, in the same way those do-it-yourself ancestry websites are doing for families the world over. During the 90s, it was discovered that sauvignon blanc and cabernet franc parented the noble cabernet sauvignon after the two were left to their own devices in a field in Bordeaux. It was also discovered that chardonnay is the offspring of pinot noir and gouais blanc, and that Italy's primitivo is the same thing as the US's zinfandel, which they also discovered is originally from Croatia. Who knew? Scandal and upset even affects viticulture; it's not just finding out who your parents are, but also who *you* are. Professor Jean-Michel Boursiquot is a French ampelographer. In 1994, Boursiquot discovered that vineyards planted with merlot in many Chilean vineyards were not in fact merlot, but carménère.

He did the same in South Australia, where he discovered vineyards that were supposed to be planted with the Spanish albariño were in fact planted with the French grape savagnin.

I was reminded of this recently when I learned more about my own family history. I always knew a bit of the story – Dutch via Indonesia on one side and English via the First Fleet on the other, with a graveyard in Tasmania to prove it. I heard other stories along the way but, as is the case with families, the truth is sometimes a hard island to come ashore on; while one recalls 'a lost gold mine as a reward for rescuing a princess in South America', another hears it as 'a prison sentence during the Mexican Revolution'.

Recently the story got much more interesting; six generations back, before Holland, before Indonesia, was Persia.

### ❦   TASTING NOTES   ❦

❦   Persia, known as Iran since 1935, has long been considered the site of the oldest evidence of winemaking in the world – up to 5500 BC – and a town there, Shiraz, is noted in the writings of many European travellers.

❧ It is also home to the legend of the discovery of wine. King Jamsheed liked to keep jars of grapes to enjoy outside of harvest. When left too long, some of the jars of grapes would start fermenting – these were thought to be poison. A young Persian girl, unhappy because of her treatment by the king, tried to take her own life by drinking the poison. Instead of death, she awoke from her alcohol-induced sleep to discover she was not only alive, but the recipient of a reward from King Jamsheed for her good discovery.

# FAVOURITES

We spend a lot of time wondering about, and feel a lot of pressure to select, our favourite things in life. Wine is no different, and I suspect the reason for this is largely out of the hope that such a vast and complex topic can be simplified to a point of absolute certainty. There are so very many possibilities, it is a relief and comfort to think there might be just one that suits us above all others.

And when you declare your favourite, who can argue? Your favourite is an untouchable thing, so adored by and connected to you, for reasons that are so unique to you, that no-one can dispute it.

I don't like picking a favourite anything, and I often feel pushed to do so. It's not that I don't love things absolutely – it's just that there are so many degrees of wonderful, there is so much in life to devour, that I don't know how you can, or why you should, reject so many for the sake of choosing one. To me, choosing a favourite feels like I'm declaring myself closed to all future possibilities of experiences, tastes and flavours. What's the point of tasting, if not with your arms wide open? It's just so restrictive. Of all the possibilities and options, moods and seasons, flavours and colours, why just one?

Can you imagine? 'No thanks,' you'll say, 'no need to show me the menu, I'm happy having this dish forever.' Or holding up an open hand and saying, 'Stop right there. I'll not have that intriguing glass of something I've never had before. This wine, which I have right here, is my favourite'? Or standing up in front of friends and family and declaring that you have found your favourite person, and for the rest of your life you will only ever be with ... Oh! ...

I know people who have chosen too quickly, perhaps when under the influence of the effects of their first heady glass. Allured by something they no longer remember, they are stuck with the decision because they declared it 'the one' too early and spend the next years trying to get out of it.

I know of someone who fell for the intense, velvety and oh-so-very-noble nature of cabernet only to realise that, when they were passed their love of the obvious, they were more fond of the savoury, earthy, lighter and more relaxed palate of a Chianti, which they first took as quiet sips on the side. And another who responded to the fun of sauvignon blanc one hot summer. But, as it was one of the first styles of wine they tasted, they didn't realise that they were too young, that there was so much more to try and that their tastes and desires would develop.

What would they drink when summer was over and it was time to eat fuller, more complex dishes, away from all that sunshine?

If I must commit, here are a few of my favourite one-and-onlys:

- To invigorate the night it is, of course, champagne. And if I must get more specific, blanc de blancs, for its fineness and precision. If it's a hot summer's day, or simply the beginning of a meal, or even just because.

- A sunny afternoon on a nice patch of grass calls for a different type of favourite – an ice-cold bottle of dry and savoury rosé, a wine that tastes as gorgeous as it looks.

- I can't go past the solid gentleness of beloved chardonnay, a refined and complex comfort.

- And, of course, there's the beautiful perfume and certain structure of pinot noir, which, when at its best, feels like you're licking wet velvet.

See? That's the lovely thing about wine: you're allowed favourites to suit every occasion, dish and season of both mind and nature. How could I possibly be expected to choose just one? Why should you? I suggest you choose so many that it becomes more like a favourite wine list than a favourite wine, which is much more appropriate, given all that life has to devour.

### 'Love, and do what you like.'

—St Augustine

## ❦ TASTING NOTES ❦

### HOW TO KEEP YOUR WINE MIND OPEN:

❦  Try new wines enthusiastically. Sample wines by the glass at
good wine bars and let sommeliers guide you.

❦  Be brave ... try things you haven't tried before. It won't be
the same as your last glass, but it might be your best yet.

❦  Think about what else you like — food, dishes, sauces, styles
of cooking — and find wines that go well with them. Help new
wines to be the best they can be by putting them in situations that
will let them shine.

---

# FLAWS

P eople are inherently flawed. It's just the way it is.

But no matter how accepting we are of the concept of being
flawed, it seems to me that we are much less tolerant of the flaws
themselves. We trawl our lives for imperfections to hide away, all
in pursuit of this elusive ideal of flawlessness. But finding flaws in
humans is as surprising as digging underground to find rocks.

So why the attraction to flawlessness?

To me, there is a neutrality to flawlessness that puts it close to
blandness. No flaws sure, but what does that mean? It's not beautiful, because beauty is moving. It's not perfect, as perfect is still
an ideal version of something. And it's not interesting, because
that's engaging.

Flawlessness without other virtues is a sort of no-man's land, a waiting room you wait in before you decide to become something. Maybe the attraction comes from the fact that being flawless was once deemed polite or appropriate.

But I still think that flaws – not faults – are to your personality what a birthmark is to your body, a mountain is to a landscape: things that make you distinctively you. It's true you may not be able to fault someone who is flawless, but it can be hard to admire them for it, too.

Some say this blandness is what has happened to some areas of winemaking in the last few decades. Technology, globalisation and new markets helped clean up winemaking, then took it a bit too far. Flaws that for centuries had been considered a part of winemaking were removed. But then people started to notice that, although the flaws were gone, so too was something else.

Hugh Johnson once wrote, 'I would rather drink a worse wine if it had more to say.' Now it seems this sentiment is being expressed by winemakers who are approaching wine with more of the idea of yin and yang, rather than the idea of cleanliness; that is, understanding that, in everything, the light exists with a dot of the dark, and vice versa, and knowing that this is not a flaw, but balance. With this view, the aim in life and winemaking is not to rid yourself of the dots, but to accept them; because even in the very best version of you, you don't exist without them.

'*Certain flaws are necessary for the whole. It would seem strange if old friends lacked certain quirks.*'

*—Goethe*

## ❦ TASTING NOTES ❦

THOUGH THERE ARE SOME VERY CLEAR FAULTS, THERE ARE
A FEW ASPECTS OF WINEMAKING THAT AROUSE DEBATE AS
TO WHETHER THEY ARE FAULTS OR FLAWS. WITHIN ALL OF
THESE, IT SEEMS IT ALL COMES DOWN TO DEGREES.
HERE ARE A FEW:

❦ Sulphides occur naturally during winemaking, and in
significant quantities they give a wine a rotten-egg smell. However,
in lower amounts they give a wine a flinty or 'struck match'
character that many people desire, and some winemakers even seek
out. What is intriguing to one is unpleasant to another.

❦ The use of whole grape bunches in winemaking, as
opposed to separating the fruit from the stems, is a traditional
winemaking technique that has seen a recent increase in
exposure. Proponents say that it adds another layer of complexity
to wine; others argue that it adds green characters to a wine,
especially if the stems are under-ripe.

❦ Brettanomyces is a yeast that, depending on who you
speak to, is a fault, a flaw or added complexity. 'Brett', as it is
commonly known, gives the wine a mousy or barnyard-y flavour,
which some people tolerate and others are repulsed by.

❦ The natural wine movement, which in itself is impossible to
define, given the degrees of naturalness available, opens a whole
new conversation. Some say these wines are natural and more
expressive of the terroir because they have no unnatural inputs;
others say that without some intervention, natural wines
can be just plain faulty.

## GARDENS

I n pursuit of a wine education over several years, I have been engaged in many activities and experiences that have helped me peel back the layers to understand the complexities and magic of wine. But of all the travel, tastings, workshops and masterclasses I have done, none have been more successful in fusing it all together than growing my own vegetable patch.

It's a slice of earth, about 6 by 10 feet, that sits between the house and the fence. Two springs ago, on an impulse, I ripped the patch up and planted a vegetable garden.

The first year, it was a thrilling bounty – well, things grew, and that was thrilling. A wall of cheeky red tomatoes sprang up, along with basil, parsley, sage, thyme, rosemary, fiery chillies, two stalks of corn, a dozen snow peas and a few other vegetables.

I was thrilled these beauties bothered to show up in the same way I'm still surprised people bother to show up for my birthday party. 'You grew for *me*?' I said to no-one, turning my head from side to side, flicking imaginary tresses off my shoulders.

I was surprised at how swiftly I lost sight of my actual contribution to this, when really, it was all nature's good work. As I dragged bemused friends into the patch to show them a capsicum the size of a berry, I realised the joy was really my own.

It was my miracle.

★        ✳        ✳        ★

✳        ★        ★

✳        ★        ★        ✳

At first the lessons were practical ones ... I learned small and functional tasks that addressed the basic objective – to grow things. Watering, weeding, fending off snails and keeping things upright. When things didn't grow well or in a normal shape – come to think of it, what *was* normal? – I accepted them adoringly anyway. I was responsible, and these were my special children. A bent capsicum or beanbag-shaped tomato were not faults – just vintage variation. When the sun did shine, I helped my chubby little tomatoes ripen by peeling back the canopy, just like I heard they did in vineyards.

That first summer was a cool one and, as I saw sheets of rain where there should have been sunrays, I noticed I was compiling my own vintage report. The weather was no longer something that just happened, but something that happened to my garden.

Whatever nature threw at me, I had to concede and work with. It was now in charge, not me – which, over time, I realised had always been the case.

I now understood why so much time was spent discussing vintage conditions in winemaking, something I had always considered a bit like a slide night of someone else's holiday – a long account fascinating only to those who were engaged in it. But when I saw the story of my own vegetables unfold (yes, we're still talking cherry tomatoes) I saw the narrative develop. 'They started off really well, with that long stint of warm weather, but remember that storm? Well they were just coming good when that hit, and there was some damage ... but mostly they came good, in the end.' Suddenly, there *was* a story – and things were, literally, at stake.

I also came to appreciate how hard it is to do something against nature's will. This also taught me to be grateful for what I did get, because sometimes it could be nothing. I had more empathy for wines from difficult vintages, just for making it through. I imagined how extraordinary the perfect vintages must be, and wondered if the celebration is as much about what did happen as what could have.

The other thing I noted about growing my own vegetables was the flavour. People who advocate home-grown vegetables talk of inconceivable aromas, texture and flavours. They don't exaggerate. Even the aromas from warm tomatoes plucked off the vine engage; the sound of a snow pea breaking is as clear as a snap of the fingers, and a tasty parsley leaf feels like a layer of lace on your tongue. I guess this is what natural wine and biodynamicists advocate: the authenticity of the original.

In the kitchen, another shift happened – rather than eat what I desired, no matter what the season or climate, I ate more around what was in season. Which also made me wonder – if it was out of season, where *was* it coming from? I started to cook more, which was a shift in itself, but it just seemed like the right thing to do. After just one season, as seasonal eating became natural, wine matching became more instinctive. When gorgeous autumnal root vegetables start roasting, a savoury earthy red becomes an obvious and beautiful match. There was less technical discussion about what goes with what; pairing became instinctive.

During the second year, with basic skills mastered, the lessons were more around the integration of things. In the second spring, I was keen to expand the range of plants – but I was reminded that you can't just grow what you want, but what is suitable. Nature has an order of where things can grow and, despite the most determined efforts, it has the final say. In some parts of the world, there is a reshuffling of wine varieties to remove those that many had wished would work, and replace them with those that are suited to the region.

In this second year, there were seasonal differences in the performance of my vegetables – but why? I started to pay attention to the detail. I noticed small idiosyncrasies of the patch; although things did grow in the corner near the fence, nothing grew *quite as well* there – the soil was slightly different than it was just a foot away, and was there less light getting through? The drainage didn't seem as good, with water pooling in heavy rains. And the breeze didn't seem so enthusiastic there. All these things, in very small ways, made a difference to the quality of my vegetables. And just like that, I classified my own patch into designations of quality, my own appellation d'origine contrôlée. Burgundy made a little more sense.

As part of my attempt to understand the performance of my patch, someone suggested I look into soil health. And, just like that, a whole other layer was revealed: soil management. To expect a discussion on soil to be a discussion on dirt is like expecting a discussion on the environment to be one about trees. Soil – its health, management, use, treatment and type – covers economics, politics, big business, philosophy, science and agriculture.

I was led into things like soil preparation, a worm farm and composting. I started saving scraps, feeding worms, stirring compost. Nothing from the garden was waste anymore. Soon after, I visited a winery where they were making compost tea – and I was more interested in that than tasting their wines.

In this second season, I began to learn of the cycle of nature. A cycle that didn't start in spring, when I planted, but a cycle that was older and more diligent, enduring and faithful than anything I know.

At one stage I sprinkled something on the garden that, according to the instructions, I shouldn't get on my skin. It made me curious how this would transform so the food that grew would be ok to eat. Yes – I guess that was the chemical farming discussion, and the same line of reasoning that leads many vineyards to seek to minimise it, even though to do so is often harder and less economical than not.

There were knock-on effects of my 'bounty' for others, as well.

I read somewhere that backyards were no longer the haven for birds they once were – larger populations, increased house sizes and a trend toward minimal landscaping all left birds with fewer habitats. So it was with joy that I welcomed visits from gangs of different birds – even if it was to feast on my tomatoes, olives and figs, not something fellow gardeners or viticulturalists encourage.

Anthropomorphising also became commonplace – to see a plant that was once bobbing happily in the breeze, flashing its fruit for you to pick, become bedraggled and wilting was like seeing the plant version of a sad face.

And when these beautiful expressions from the garden faded toward spoilage, I thought instinctively about saving them – literally preserving them. Like throwing out your own art, throwing out my garden felt personal.

*       *       *       *

*           *           *

*           *           *           *

Eventually, the lessons became larger and were often just observations of awe … there were the small joys – such as wakening one morning to see a fig branch dotted with bright-green, fluffy shoots – which make you feel part of something exciting and that, no matter what, life will be just fine. This was my very own budburst and I came to appreciate the overwhelming sense of progress and husbandry that viticulturalists must feel every spring when their vines do the same thing. Not to mention the thrill of seeing acres and acres of such new growth.

I marvelled at how this garden grew so generously, when we seem to be so careless to the rest of nature. To see bright, bold fruit and vegetables growing near tall buildings and housing developments seemed to me the kindest thing an organism could do.

I also pondered: if it could be this spectacular in a small patch at the hand of a hack in an inner-city block, what would be possible on a larger scale when done well? I mean, could you – could you *really* live off the land?

Now, when the garden is unkempt or whittled down to a hardy herb or two, I feel like I am being unproductive and wasteful and that I am letting something down.

What that thing *is*, I am not sure. Perhaps it's the same thing that people have been trying to explain and pay a worthy tribute to for centuries, that thing that connects us with something special and secret and more magnificent and grand than anything I have come to know: nature.

*'I can think of no better form of personal involvement in the cure of the environment than that of gardening.'*

—Wendell Berry

# GENEROSITY

I have a friend who is a big and generous personality. Not big in a serial-pest way, but in a fill-the-room-with-energy way. My friend turns a nice dinner into an outrageous event, fills pesky silences with fun commentary and turns dull conversations into a livelier version of themselves. When my friend barrels into a room, it fills up with noise and chatter and gutsy laughter. Sure, small birds scatter out of trees, cats hide under floors and piano players stop, but things do get brighter.

For me, a wine is made much more enjoyable when consumed in a spirit of generosity. I can't think of anything that sucks more out of the enjoyment of a glass of wine than a constant attitude of frugalness. I have experienced it in many guises: someone knowingly going to a dinner party with the cheapest bottle of wine and drinking three of the host's finest, people slicing restaurant bills down to the various glasses of wine, drinkers sitting in on a shout then dodging theirs with a lame 'I'm driving'.

It's not just in their approach to wine but in their entire approach to life that certain people pinch and scrimp and sit on the sidelines and live less joyfully than is possible. Their approach to food and wine is just one expression of this. These types travel through life as passengers, waiting for others to create opportunities – be they chances for fun, work, or love – that they usually take from but rarely contribute to. They may believe they are the victims of bad fortune in life, that anyone else's joy is merely good luck. If only they realised they were receiving the exact amount of fortune they created for themselves.

But, though it certainly makes way for it, an absence of

frugalness does not always equate to a spirit of generosity. To my mind, a spirit of generosity is not to be mixed with excess or gluttony or showy displays of wealth. A spirit of generosity is not the same as buying from the top of the wine list with scant appreciation for anything but bragging rights. It's as much about a generous attitude to your wine, food and friends – even if there are consequences for small and surrounding animals. It's about having enough curiosity about the good things in life to peek behind the curtain – and when you do, knowing it's worth every cent for the sake of your pleasure alone.

'Enjoy life. There's plenty of time to be dead.'

—Hans Christian Andersen

## GEWÜRZTRAMINER

Appropriateness and I have had a chequered relationship, especially when it comes to wearing the right outfit at the right time. Of course I'll behave and shine at a wedding in whatever costume the bride prescribes but, at less directed events, I like to choose outfits according to how I feel or where I wish I

## PERFUME IN A GLASS

Gewürztraminer is famous for its Alsatian versions, but is made all around the world, especially well in Germany and New Zealand. When done right, she has a perfume of rose, lychee and musk; less attractive versions of gewürztraminer have these notes but with less balance and precision – as if she'd applied her make-up in a moving car.

was, not where I actually am. As a result, I have been known to dress up and down at all the wrong times: for a safari when heels and sequins are in order, or for a night on the town at a small person's christening. It just makes me feel a little bit special.

Gewürztraminer, the white wine with the exotic name, is a drop that some say also has a tendency to over-dress. Hardly her fault. She was just born oozing a wafty perfume of rose, lychee, musk, a sprinkling of spice and an occasional tropical fruit. She's just as enthusiastic on the palate as well, an unctuous and oily mouthful of flavour with a hint of spice.

Too much? Not so. Take the wafty perfume head to head and pair gewürztraminer with a banquet of Thai food, perhaps the single most aromatic cuisine on earth; it's a mix of aromas that will make a department-store perfume hall envious. Sure she's got some perfume, but that's ok. Sometimes, with wine as with life, a girl needs to feel a little bit special.

## ❦  TASTING NOTES  ❦

### THE IDEAL LUNCHEON WINE

❦  Luncheon wines are usually white (but sometimes pink) wines that err toward lower alcohol and are all about being gentle, delicate and unobtrusive – definitely not heady wines. Riesling, pinot gris, pinot grigio, gewürztraminer or even a savoury rosé all make excellent luncheon wines.

❦  Typically, luncheons include fewer courses and lighter dishes, so wines should be paired to match. What's more, a luncheon usually requires at least some output by the diner in the afternoon, so everything should be kept in check; keep yourself tidy, as it were.

# GLASSWARE

There is a lot of talk about wine glasses, otherwise known as stemware, and it would be easy to simplify it and dismiss it as an unnecessary piece of wine puffery, but wine glasses do make a difference. Of course the difference is subtle and pleasing rather than practical and enduring. Good glasses make a difference in the way writing with a fountain pen is different from writing with a plastic one, or the way soft leather gloves are different from wearing fleece gloves. They're not only more effective; they make the act more special.

To understand the impact the size or shape of a glass has on a wine, consider how the size of a stage affects a performer. To put

## THE FRENCH DISH

Legend has it that the champagne saucer, also known as the champagne coupe – that shallow bowl-like glass that you see at weddings and on the recycled timber shelves of vintage collectors – was modelled on the breast of champagne loving strumpet Marie Antoinette. Regardless, the champagne saucer is not the preferred vessel for enjoying champagne or sparkling wine; the wide surface area means the bubbles dissipate quickly and the very gentle aromas are lost.

a delicate, petite and perfectly trained ballerina onto a huge, gaping, cavernous stage is to ask the impossible of a performer whose skill and specialisation is in filling up a small space beautifully, wonderfully, perfectly. The opposite is also true: put a symphony orchestra with the largesse and ability to produce loud, significant, complex sounds on your back veranda and see how much noise is made and how much music is lost. Different wine glasses are designed to allow different wines to express themselves properly.

❧    TASTING NOTES    ❧

FOLLOW A FEW BASIC RULES TO GIVE YOUR WINE
THE PERFORMANCE OF ITS LIFE:

❧  Aim for clear glass with no embellishments so you can see the clarity and quality of the wine.

❧  A tulip shape in which the aromas of the swirled wine can kick up and still be captured for your pleasure is a good option.

❧  Look for a stemmed glass, so that the heat from your hand doesn't warm your wine.

❦  If you can splash out, get a smaller glass for whites, larger for
   reds and a flute for your bubbles.

# GLUTTONY

T hroughout the dinner the four of us ate very well, and generously: several plates to share for entrees, and for mains full
dishes with salads, bread and butter. As the meal progressed from
lighter to heavy, so too did the wines, from champagne to chablis
to something dark and exotic. The waiter came over to ask if he
could 'offer a little dessert or perhaps some cheese'. We looked
guiltily at each other. We had declared ourselves full about a dish
and a half ago. Politely, we said yes, we'd take two of the sweet
things and a plate of cheese – and why not throw in a sticky dessert
wine to complete the match and finish the job properly?

We knew it to be too much, but we figured we could just have a
nibble and leave any we didn't want.

Couldn't we?

In the taxi on the way home, as I sighed and loosened the belt
on my jeans, I began to wonder. Did I have this all wrong? Was this
excess a sign of being gastronomically accomplished and having
reached a point of joie de vivre – a true epicurean, as it were? Or
was I being a gluttonous and wasteful food heathen, destined for
nothing but hellfire and damnation?

What *is* the difference between gluttony and gastronomical
passion? And is one more right or better than the other?

★        ✻        ✻        ★

  ✻        ★        ★

✻        ★        ★        ✻

Whether the idea of gluttony *started* in religion is still uncertain, but it was eventually included in Christian teachings. Gluttony was considered a sin because excessive consumption of food by one meant less for others; during times of food scarcity, this is understandably poor behaviour.

Medieval theologian Thomas Aquinas, somewhat of a trainspotter for gluttony, took the idea further and broke it down into different types of gluttony. At my gluttonous dinner, according to Aquinas I sinned at least with both *laute* (eating too expensively) and *nimis* (eating too much). And I promise I have revelled without care in the other kinds as well.

But scanning through history, it seems that whether overindulgence is a sin or a sign of status is all a matter of culture. While some religious types thought it deprived the poor, the Romans felt indulgence was a display of wealth; lavish feasting was an important activity for members of Roman society. Tales of such feasts sparked legends about the mythical vomitorium, an alleged bathroom-like space that overly satiated Romans visited to relieve themselves by vomiting.

Though gluttony might be a matter of culture, it seems we have always been suspicious of the pursuit of pleasure, when in doubt pushing it towards a sin rather than a sign of a life well-lived. The philosopher Epicurus, who was actually concerned with pleasure as a way to avoid human suffering, came to represent justification for the lowest forms of debauchery.

These days, I think an intimate and authentic pleasure is often missed in the pursuit of box-ticking one's way down the list of top restaurants and great wines. This is a sort of superficiality, rather than gluttony, just as eating bad food gluttonously is less about gluttony than thoughtlessness.

I can see how fervent eating and drinking might be considered as some kind of weakness, but I think there is a bit more to it. The enjoyment and conscious appreciation of food and wine is one of the more enlightened and respectful things you can do with wine and food.

And I'll admit, I do wonder if to truly enjoy wine and food is to be a little gluttonous. I get pleasure from excess; it's like being as adoring and passionate as you can be. The more you enjoy wine, the more there is to enjoy – wine of all kinds, from all places, from old and new vintages and vineyards. To enjoy so much I think is just being enthusiastic, and is something more akin to passion than debauchery.

So, I guess, if enthusiasm for pleasure is a sin, and a delight in excess is gluttony, then yes, I am guilty.

## ❦  TASTING NOTES  ❦

❦  Gluttony was considered one of the Seven Deadly Sins, the others being lust, sloth, envy, wrath, pride and greed.

❦  St Gregory the Great, a pope from the Middle Ages, and Thomas Aquinas expanded on the idea and broke gluttony into sub-categories. You don't want these guys planning your party.

❦ Thomas's list of types of gluttony included 'praepropere', eating too soon; 'laute', eating too expensively; 'nimis', eating too much; 'ardenter', eating too eagerly; 'studiose', eating too daintily, and 'forente', eating wildly.

❦ The list of sub-sins for Gregory the Great included eating before meals, looking for better quality of food to please your tastes, seeking sauces and seasonings for the enjoyment of your palate, eating too much food, and eating with too much enthusiasm.

❦ Despite his modern reputation as a civilised excuse for excess, Epicurus was actually against excess, debauchery or gluttony, and for a happy life, free from pain or suffering.

---

# GOD OF THE GAPS

When it comes to nature, mankind has struggled to believe that things just happen. Rather, we like to believe they happen because there is something deeper or more spiritual at work.

Early man was particularly good at this, attributing gods to just about anything that could not be explained. To explain the presence and actions of the sun, storms, mountains, rivers, moon, winds and sea, the ancient Egyptians, Indians, Chinese and Greeks all had stories and deities. Often they were anthropomorphised, given names, narratives and customs.

We were then, as we are now, a tribe of wanton storytellers.

Some have called this the God of the Gaps: wherever there was something that could not be explained, a god was invented to explain it.

I can see why you might consider this; I mean, imagine trying to make sense of the world and its natural and often ruthless cycles. How could you think a raging inferno was the work of anything other than someone who was very angry? A field of flowers in spring anything other than a gift from something larger than you? Or, when witnessing the ghost-like shimmer of a gust of wind dance across the ocean, how could you think it anything other than the work of a spirit? Assigning meaning to such wonders helps us to make sense of and give thanks to a rather curious world.

Greek mythology was particularly well known for creating a tribe of gods to explain the world, including Dionysus, the god of wine, later known to the Romans as Bacchus.

Dionysus was invented to express all that was mystical about wine and, at a time when there were no labs or textbooks, there was a lot of mystery. Dionysus was there to explain the fluctuation in harvests, wine's mood-altering properties and the variations in grapes, and he was the guy to thank for the completion of one harvest and to pray to for the continuity of another. Unlike many other gods, who remained mythical and intangible, Dionysus was even more special because you were in fact able to drink him.

Although intoxication from Dionysus was considered a good thing and was celebrated, rage and madness were also acknowledged, perhaps to symbolise other sides of intoxication.

Dionysus, despite his might and influence, was eventually made redundant like other gods of the gaps. At first it was through the forerunner of Christianity, which deemed the celebrations in his honour inappropriate places of crime and conspiracy, and then science did away with him.

We now have some pretty clear evidence as to what really makes grapes turn into wine, why varieties taste like they do and why some crops are better than others; we even know how to encourage growth, protect against disease and add bubbles. What Dionysus was responsible for over thousands of years, we can now learn in three years at university.

Or can we?

You see, despite our technological advances and degrees – what we can see under a microscope and taste in our glass – there is still a pleasant amount of mystery in wine.

Winemakers are frequently at a loss to explain many aspects of the winemaking process. We still can't protect against the weather or control disease, and we have no way ever of explaining why wine can make us feel and think what we do. There's still a lot that science can't account for.

A good thing, as this is one of the charms and allure of wine.

So, depending on what you believe, maybe the gods are long gone. But thankfully, the mystery isn't.

## GOLDEN AGE OF WINE

I like to go back and hang out in other times and experience other eras. I explore them by reading books, ensconcing myself in a landscape or, from time to time, sporting inappropriate outfits, just to get in the mood – the pith helmet, when considering a safari, was a case in point.

It's not so much a dissatisfaction with today – although I do wonder if we have it right – but more a curiosity and wonder with other times. There are so many golden ages lost to us that I would love to explore. The golden age of conversation in 16th-century France, when salons were a major part of civilised society; the golden age of safari, with Osa and Martin Johnson (although I am utterly and entirely against game hunting); the golden age of travel, when wilderness was abundant and traces of man hard to find; the golden age of sail, where flotillas of tall ships carried cargo from other worlds. And of course, the mystical golden age, from which proponents believe everything – people, life, society, values – has been deteriorating ever since.

I often ask people this question in relation to wine: If you could live in any time in history for wine – from the Big Wine Bang until now – when would it be? The exciting thing is, everyone says right now. That's right, enjoy, people; we're in the halcyon days of wine.

This is refreshing given that, outside of wine, I don't think many people would say the same thing; we're told that unless we turn the ship around, important things are going to get worse.

It's not unusual to romanticise the past; people have done so for centuries. Many worship Paris in the 20s; the Stoic philosophers thought the simplicity of the 'golden age' was superior; the ancient Greeks thought those that came before had simpler, more natural lives; and many people today, caught in a busy cycle of consumption, wish for another time. Is the tree change a modern cultural primitivism? Perhaps.

But most people say that today is the best time for wine at any point in history. Isn't that exciting? There are many reasons for this, although I can't help but wonder if one reason we are experiencing the halcyon days of wine is because a lot of winemakers are turning back the clock on the way they make wine. Maybe Wendell Berry was right: 'When looking back makes sense, you are going ahead.'

*'The golden age is before us, not behind us.'*

—William Shakespeare

❦  TASTING NOTES  ❦

WHY NOW MIGHT BE THE BEST TIME
IN THE HISTORY OF WINE:

❦  Great wine is made all around the world – not just in
traditional Old World countries like France and Italy, but in
Chile, Argentina, Australia and New Zealand, not to mention
re-emerging countries such as those in the Balkans.

❦  We have the benefits of technology, and some
of the wisdom of experience.

❦  Though there is lively debate around it, there are signs of an
alternative way of looking at agriculture: we are now seeing the
effects of chemical farming, and many don't like it. At the very
least, the conversation is alive.

❦  There is a diversity of varieties being nurtured and cultivated,
and a diversity of winemaking philosophies.

❦  We have the benefit – some more than others – of the
experience of place. Those newer regions that have less of it have
much to look forward to.

Wine is pretty much available to most and, as a result of all these
points, there is high-quality, interesting and
authentic wine at all prices.

# GOOD WINE - WHAT IS IT?

'Oh, you write about *wine*? You'd know then: what's a good wine?'

It always takes me by surprise. Huh? Me? A *good* wine? I know what they mean, of course I do. They ask what a good wine is because they, like most people, think there's a room that they don't have access to but that you do. And that inside this room all the answers are written on the walls, and that you'll let them be your plus-one into this sanctum of wine wisdom.

Which is fair enough. For many people, there is an intrinsic message hidden in the bottom drawer of wine connoisseurship that suggests that in order to enjoy wine, you really should know something about it.

You also know that what they're really asking for is a solution in the form of a remarkable wine recommendation that will help to cut through all the 'stuff'; a wine so extraordinary that when it is opened, it will launch the first firework of a spectacular *son et lumière* show, underneath which a parade of floats led by unicorns will roll by, and balloons and confetti will fall from the sky, gently brushing their smiling cheeks and blinking eyelashes.

It's a stunning question because it's difficult to answer in the same way your favourite-ever anything is hard to list in three seconds.

Three seconds: what's your favourite movie *ever*? Album? Book? See?

Wine is the same; a good wine according to *what*? What do you normally drink? What do you like? At what price point? For when? What food do you like? What do you believe in? Who are you drinking with? Buying for?

Sure, I can tell you some good wines, but the question is bigger than that. I have wondered, I mean, seriously, what *is* a good wine? And why is that question so hard to answer? So I asked around and, of course, it's not very straightforward.

## GOOD ACCORDING TO WINE SHOWS

Wine-show judges use a set of parameters to judge whether a wine is good – and not just that it is good, but *how* good. These parameters include things like the appropriate tinges and hues; an aroma or bouquet that is indicative of the wine's variety or style; and the use of oak and its integration into the wine. Further attributes include a well-balanced palate, lack of bitterness and a long and pleasing after-palate. Wines should also show typicity of variety and region. As you'd expect, gold-medal and trophy wines need to go that bit further and deliver an extra level of quality: more finesse, better structure and better finish. But, while agricultural show judging is about 'improving the breed', some say the system is flawed and not necessarily an indication of what makes a good wine for a normal drinking occasion. Some even call them wet T-shirt contests – you know, only the most obvious, not the most stylish or creative, wins.

## TAKE A STAND

There is another school of thought, which seems to be growing in voice and number, that says a wine's quality has for too long focused on technical attributes. Some believe that technology has asserted too much control, taking out the natural expression of some wine, its character, style and sense of place. Suddenly, goes the argument, there were cases of wines that were a bit like the potential mate who is perfect on paper, but in person lacks character no matter how hard you try to love them. Just as we get bored with faultlessness or perfection in people, it seems we get bored of it in wine as well. Many believe good wines are those that express something, whether we like it or not. For a wine to be good in this camp, it's about having authenticity, character, having stood for something.

## Philosophically speaking

Well, it was always going to come up: the inevitable disclaimer that argues that because we're human, everything is subjective, including wine; it's just the way we're built. Of course, there's truth in this. Our palates vary, environmental conditions change, tasting with food changes everything, and there are the emotional states that can change how we taste, meaning that no matter how strict the conditions, there will be always be ... subjectivity.

It's not just the physical or emotional aspects that influence our perceptions. There are also those highly personal things in a wine that move us, whether we are aware of it or not. Perhaps a good wine is one that speaks for us when we can't find the words, or makes the offering that we are unable to. Maybe a good wine is one that takes a stand as we wish we could, like our heroes do in our favourite novels. Maybe a good wine expresses a value that we can relate to, like the first time you lock eyes with your tribe in high school, realising that finally, you belong somewhere. These are legitimate things that make anything good – people choose husbands and wives over such gestures. Why not wine?

Some philosophers question whether you can even tell if anything is good with certainty. The way to do this is the process that the Greeks called *aethesis*, from which the word 'aesthetic' comes, meaning 'perception by means of the senses'. This is the process we know if tasting and assessing consciously. But if two wine judges taste the same wine and come to different conclusions, who is to say who is right? Many philosophers say this comes down to a matter of taste, and that you can never know for certain if something is good. For philosophers, this issue of taste seems to be the final word. Or, put another way, *de gustibus non est disputandum*, 'tastes are not disputable'. Maybe it ends here: it's just a matter of taste. Therefore, *that's* a good wine. End of discussion.

Fine, except someone forgot to send the memo to the wine industry.

## 'I rather like bad wine ...
## one gets so bored with good wine.'

—Benjamin Disraeli

### ETHICALLY GOOD

What if the issue is not so much about what makes a wine good but what, indeed, makes *anything* good? A difficult thing to pin down, given what is deemed 'good' has been changing regularly since time began. Some believe society is going through a paradigm shift from a greedy period of consumption to being moral consumers, redeeming ourselves for wrongs committed and seeking absolution for our previous consumer choices. This is a reaction against the heady, showy, badge-hungry days of the 80s and 90s, when luxury purchases were a personal right, Paris was a superstar, not a city, and bottled water was a sensible invention. What we think is a good choice today has shifted. You can see this in wine as well. Moral, ethical and environmental issues in winemaking are discussed. Many are talking about natural winemaking, hand-crafting wine and listening to nature. More are exploring biodynamic winemaking, sustainable viticulture, permaculture, indigenous varieties and less harmful packaging.

It seems now that it is not just the quality of the wine that makes it good, but the values that underpin the techniques used in its creation. On this, most agree. It's just the set of values that *make* it good that continue to divide.

Wine is complex, we knew that. But there is something in this complexity, something unique and egalitarian – if you want to talk technically, discussing minutiae of sub-regions and style, there's good wine for you. If you want to just guzzle and enjoy it, well here's cheers to the thousand good wines for that. If you want to take an ethical stand and advocate on behalf of nature, well, there's wine for that also. And if you want a wine that sets off the first firework of a spectacular *son et lumière* show, take comfort: there is good wine for that too.

Perhaps we should worry less about what makes a good wine good and think more about what makes wine good, no matter what you believe in. Even after all that, my answer – if you are still standing near me and awake – is the same: 'It depends.'

## 🍇 TASTING NOTES 🍇

🍇 Faultless: A good wine will be free from faults, but it still might have other things that some call flaws.

🍇 Balance: None of the component parts of a wine should stand out of balance with the others. Look for the integration and balance of oak, acid, fruit, tannin or sweetness.

🍇 Length: The aromas and flavours of a good wine will last, even beyond swallowing.

🍇 Typicity: Varieties should taste of themselves, even when taking into account regional, vintage or winemaker variations.

🍇 Complexity: Simplicity is not a virtue for the great. As Dorothy Parker famously quipped about Katherine Hepburn, 'She runs the gamut of emotions, from A to B.' Good wines should be complex.

🍇 Sense of place: Many look for evidence of the wine's region or origins in the wine to consider it truly good.

🍇 Taste: Do you personally like it? Whether others do or even whether they think it is good will vary from person to person.

🍇 Ethics: Does it support your values? Sure, this is getting into some more philosophical parameters, but for many they count toward the final decision.

# GREECE

To say wine is evident in Greek culture is putting things a little casually. Wine has been entrenched in Greek history for thousands of years, and we're not talking about vague and tenuous links to cultivate a deeper wine pedigree. The Greeks took wine very seriously indeed – and there are a number of traditions that show just how much.

The *symposium*, which literally means 'to drink together', was one of the most important social customs for men, and was essentially an event held to drink wine and discuss various philosophical dilemmas of the day in various degrees of seriousness. Sometimes you had Plato, other times you had girls playing flutes. At such events, men would lay about, someone would take the floor to talk and wine boys, who were effectively slave waiters, poured wine from amphorae for the guests as discussions and drinking rolled merrily along. *Libations*, an offering of wine to the gods or any other named subject, were sprinkled at the symposia.

Wine was also important for Greek philosopher Hippocrates, known as the father of medicine. Wine was a huge part of his practice and many of his remedies used wine as one of the ingredients.

## To drink together again

Greek wine is currently having a renaissance. Which seems strange, given all this history, but for the past few centuries Greece's wine industry suffered after years of political distraction, war and emigration. Now a range of climates, more than three hundred indigenous varieties, seven regions, old vineyards, and the benefit of tradition mixed with modernity are making Greece one of the most exciting regions to watch … well, for at least another few thousand years.

Then there's Greek literature, where the works of the ancient Greek writer Homer are riddled with talk of wine, such as the Wine-Dark Sea, which some say refers to the Aegean Sea, a flourishing wine region at the time. If this is not commitment enough, the Greeks also dedicated an entire God – Dionysus – to the magical drop.

## GRÜNER VELTLINER

I was having dinner in a small bistro with a special friend who was in town for a wedding. The last time I saw her was in London, her current home, before and after my visit to France last year.

Whenever we're together, we bombard each other with intense and thoughtful discussions about life and all its joys and complexities. These conversations are, for us, one of life's joys, and at times one of its complexities. We understand each other's successes and messes and unique perspectives on the world, and our time together has helped me invent my own views on life.

For example, after encouraging each other to leap between careers, countries and experiences over the last decade, I am convinced that you should try everything and go everywhere you want to – because experience is not gained by reliving the same year twenty times over. I have also realised there are many poorly designed and outdated concepts still circulating as the dominant model. Their dominance doesn't make them good, just ubiquitous – so if the model doesn't fit, don't sign up. Or, better still, create your own version.

And I've learned that, despite what society says, there are few deadlines that are real deadlines; mostly the noise is made up of small pressures from another time. Ignore them if you want to. Take your time if you need to.

Come to think of it, our catch-ups are part salon, part dinner.

She handed the wine list to me. 'You choose,' she said. 'And then tell me something about it.'

I chose a grüner veltliner. 'It's grown mostly in Austria but it's spreading to the New World. It's very buzzy right now – sommeliers love it.' I knew this would appeal to her voracious appetite for emerging trends, which is a part of what she does for a living for one of the coolest companies on the planet. 'But aside from that, it's actually a great variety. All dry and crisp, sort of minerally, herbal and spicy, fabulous with food. A gorgeous way to start.'

It was lovely. We were excited about it, sommelier included.

She reminded me of a request she'd made in a bar in London last year, after I returned from France invigorated by wine and life – to give her a mini lesson on wine.

'Just a quick one,' she said, looking at her glass of grüner veltliner again – a variety she now loved, I suspect, not just for its flavour but also because she experienced a little more of the magic of wine discovery.

### AUSTRIA'S RISING WINE STAR

Grüner veltliner is a variety that was mostly grown in Austria and, to a lesser degree, Hungary. Recently, as the variety's virtues have been noted, Australia and New Zealand are also starting to take strides with the wine. A white variety, it has all the wonderful attributes of riesling – acid, sparkle and gentle aromatics – mixed with a lovely spiciness and savoury flavour which, as you might imagine, make it a wonderful wine to have with food.

'Really? Here?'

'I just want to know more about it.'

'Darl, asking for a quick lesson on wine is like asking for a quick lesson on life.'

'Perfect, I'll take both.'

We laughed. And I got to thinking – what I would say if I had to give a quick lesson on wine?

So, although there are many who know better, and more, here are my thoughts.

- Don't drink only with wine people. Not because of the clichés or caricatures – these are mostly irrelevant now – but because they will make you nervous no matter how much they say, 'If you like it, that's all that matters.' Learn from experts, and taste in casual company; eventually the best parts of the two will merge.

- If you want to learn about pinot noir, taste only pinot noir to understand all its variations. Trying to learn about pinot by comparing it to shiraz is like getting a lesson to show that red is different from blue.

- Ask questions, especially of winemakers. They're generally too humbled by Mother Nature and passionate about what they do to be anything but welcoming. No-one minds; in fact, they love to talk.

- Re-try your preferences and aversions often – things change. The wine in your glass is only one part of the story; go to the place, taste the food and talk to people if you want to find out the other parts.

- Like you would a friend, look for the good in the wine – don't always seek out the faults. The wine has things to say; listen to how you react to them, that's the right answer.

Oh, and one last thing: if you are stuck on anything – in life or wine – remember that everything and nothing matters. Especially if you find someone who you can share your joys, messes and a nice glass of wine with.

*'Friendship is born at that moment when one person says to another: "What! You too? I thought I was the only one."'*

—C.S. Lewis

## HILLS

H ills are sacred in winemaking, providing the precious land-scapes from which the world's special vineyards grow, like the silent walls that bear the great portraits of the world.

As with everything in wine, this is not an absolute rule – not all of the great wines come from hills – but they certainly contribute to many of the great wines. There's the Hermitage Hill in France's Northern Rhone; the hills surrounding Piedmont – the word means 'foot of the mountain' – which make the beautiful barolo and barbaresco wines; the steep slopes of the Mosel that express the austere German rieslings; the sloping hills of Alsace; the terraced vineyards in the Douro Valley of Portugal; and South Australia's Adelaide Hills.

Generally, hills are a welcome sight to anyone in winemaking except the pickers. The benefits of hills to viticulture have been recognised for centuries with the saying 'Bacchus loves the hills', in reference to the Roman wine god, Bacchus.

## ❦ TASTING NOTES ❦

### Vineyards on hills bring many benefits to vines:

❦    In marginal climates, the extra sunlight helps to ripen the grapes.

❦    In warmer places the extra height helps to cool the fruit, since temperature drops with height.

❦    Vines on hills benefit from better air circulation.

❦    The soil on slopes has better drainage than the more densely packed soil at ground level, which can get waterlogged or become too fertile, creating too much vine vigour and an excess of energy production and imbalanced vine.

❦    Vines at higher altitudes have to work a little harder – and, as we know, vines thrive on a little tough love.

# HOW TO LIVE

'D rink within five years.' 'Will benefit from careful cellaring for twenty years.' 'Enjoy with roast beef.' 'Serve slightly chilled or at room temperature.'

These pithy instructions on the back of a wine bottle, said to be written by the winemaker (whether or not they are), are there innocently enough to help you get the very best from your wine, knowing it was made, how well it ages and other general considerations. To enjoy a wine's full potential, these recommendations are worth considering.

If the wine were a person, these recommendations would be like getting advice on how to live well and meet your own potential. Which is not such a weird idea: many people over the years have spent time pondering what a life well-lived looks like. 'I went to the woods because I wished to live deliberately,' wrote Thoreau. He was not the first, nor will he be the last, to be consumed by this problem. History is filled with curious minds exploring the idea of a life well-lived and, as a result, hundreds of thousands of words have been written on the subject; it's any wonder we're not experts at living well.

Through all the writings, the most consistent theme seems to be that you can't live well until you're prepared to die. This reminds me a bit of the cycle of wine, because to enjoy a wine is to end it; its pleasure can't exist without its end. I think this is a lovely reminder – whether you're enjoying a bottle of wine or planning your life well-lived – that it's what comes in the middle that is the most important, and that you can't have the middle until you get to the end: And not, as Thoreau feared, 'when I came to die, discover that I had not lived.'

'*Don't cry because it's over,
smile because it happened.*'

—*Dr Seuss*

## INVISIBLE THINGS

Although I have tried to understand and know what it is, I struggle to express that *something* that enchants and bewitches us and makes us fall in love with wine.

Flavour, variety, diversity, suitability, nature, gastronomy, sociability, drunkenness – I'm sure all these things contribute, but I doubt it's just one or all of the components. If the perfect food-and-wine match creates an elusive and magical third flavour, then wine's virtues combined create a whole other universe of wonder.

I always used to think that, despite the passion that people show towards wine, it was ridiculous to try to express this with a tasting note, a punchy five-word descriptor or, worse, a number.

But as I have moved through life, I have realised that perhaps the wine world is no more guilty of this than the rest of our culture. In every major component of our lives we are moved by the invisible, yet we capture it with the tangible. Love is formalised with a marriage, faith with a contract, wisdom with a university degree, commitment with a mortgage, and freedom with a quick holiday.

And it's easy, I think, as you get older, for the tangible things to take up more space than the intangible things that moved us in the first place. But these material things – as worthy expressions of passion as they are – can also deviate from the original desire, banishing the very thing you so honourably tried to capture in the beginning.

You know, just because the invisible things are impossible to see doesn't mean they are any less important; in fact, I've come to believe they are the *most* important.

So, as we move through life, I think we need to work harder to make space for the invisible things, starting with the pleasure that comes with a bottle of wine. Just take a few seconds before you make your judgement on the wine and write your note or give it a score; while you may not be able to see the invisible things, if you take a moment, you will be able to feel them.

*'And above all, watch with glittering eyes the whole world around you because the greatest secrets are always hidden in the most unlikely places. Those who don't believe in magic will never find it.'*

—*Roald Dahl,* The Minpins

## LA DOLCE VITA

'Can I help you?' asked the bottle shop assistant.

I hoped so. I wanted to buy a wine that would take me away. Not just to any old place but to Italy, somewhere I've only been once but, with so many exciting wines spilling from its rocky shores and off its rolling hills, I have renewed interest in.

It's fair to say that Italy is one of the world's favourite wine-producing countries right now, thanks to a huge geographical diversity, a dazzling range of varieties, twenty regions and a recent evolution of its wine industry. And, of course, Italy is Italian.

I figured, if wines really do speak of their place, then wine buying is a lot like armchair travelling; an intimate taste of somewhere else that you might not have access to right at that moment. To me, I was after wines that were what Paul Theroux's *Great Railway Bazaar* is to someone contemplating a long train journey. Well, maybe not quite as definitive as that, but something to give me a hint of Italy's vinous magic.

Of course, that's not what I asked for – I didn't want to appear unhinged to the wine store salesguy, so I took a more conservative approach. I asked if he could give me directions to the Italian aisle. It wasn't quite Italy, but it was a start.

## ❧ Tasting notes ❧

❧ Prosecco, the sparkling Italian wine from the Veneto region, is becoming increasingly popular as a casual drink that offers a dry, light and fresh glass of sparkles.

❧ Vermentino, the light white from Liguria and Tuscany, produces a racy and mouth-watering drink, perfect for summer afternoons with a generous serve of seafood.

❧ Pinot grigio, the Italian version of the French pinot gris, makes a lighter and livelier white wine than its French cousin. It comes most famously from the Friuli and Alto Adige regions of Italy.

❧ Barolo and barbaresco, made from the nebbiolo grape in the Northern Piedmont region, are two of the most lauded red wines in the world for their intense and alluring perfume, structure and ability to age.

❧ Chianti and Brunello di Montalcino, made mostly from sangiovese in Tuscany, offer complexity, savouriness and earthiness.

❧ The dark and spicy nero d'Avola from dry and warm Sicily is gaining recognition for its ability to withstand hot, dry climates and produce a delightfully fragrant and savoury wine.

*'Better than a face lift, to stay young we need to be permanently in a state of intellectual curiosity.'*

—Salvador Pániker

# MANIFESTO
## TO THE WONDERS OF WINE

THIS MUCH I KNOW:

- A wine rarely starts with its first vintage.

- Wine has been made continuously around the world for over seven thousand years and is still fashionable; that is quite extraordinary.

- We will never know everything about wine, so stay curious and keep looking.

- There is a lot about wine and life that we don't understand — and this makes them better than if we knew everything.

- It is only wine, but it is *wine*.

- Good glassware improves things.

- As a wine drinker, I think the pursuit of information is admirable, but on its own, not quite right. Pleasure and beauty are arguably more worthy pursuits.

- While the information is in the details of wine, I am convinced the answers lie elsewhere.

The things that move us in wine are rarely the technical or measurable; allow those things to move you.

Wine without context is like a person without a backstory.

Age softens things, but doesn't make what is inherently there disappear.

To have a glass of wine is to have much more than a glass of wine.

I don't know if connoisseurship is noble, but whatever it is we're looking for makes it feel like it is.

The actual liquid of wine is only part of the beauty of wine; the rest is in what it allows us to imagine.

The connection people have to wine, and the connection wine has to nature, may be more important than we currently know.

Nothing throughout time has been linear except the idea of time itself; we are neither doomed nor destined for advancement. Inappropriate winegrowing progress can be reversed and current beauties expanded, if we choose.

Wine is one way of making the beautiful and the mysterious tangible.

It is still, as it always has been, what's on the inside of you, me and a bottle of wine that counts.

With wine as with life, it's what comes in the middle that is the most important; and you can't have the middle until you get to the end.

# MARITIME

W e were somewhere in the middle of the Tasman Sea, four thousand metres above the ocean floor, on a yacht bound for New Zealand from Australia when the gale hit us: an invisible wind force that engulfs and wrestles you in its snarl until it passes or dissipates. This was not unusual for this ocean. Captain Cook called the Tasman 'confused' – influenced by two competing weather patterns, it lacks the consistency and order of other seas. On a racing yacht you could try to outrun a front, but we were built for comfort, not speed, so we trimmed and battened as it swallowed us.

Up on deck, even half lying down, braced against the cabin, I had to work to keep my balance. Trying not to get seasick, between fat sprays of water drumming my face, eyes squinting from the sun's glare, I tried to hold the horizon line in my gaze as it bobbed behind the heaving swells.

The swell was four metres, the wind thirty-five knots; nothing, I was told, for ocean sailors. The only calm came in the fleeting moments when the yacht freefell off a wave: one, two, maybe three floating seconds before it smashed back onto the ocean. The harrowing wind blew across the tops of the waves, gnashing and crumbling the crest backwards. With just a little imagina-tion, the ocean of bent waves became a sea of wolves' heads, ears peeled back, jostling, dripping with saliva and ready to attack.

Only two weeks earlier I had agreed, with all the consideration of a stray dog before it jumps on the back of a truck, to be the fourth of four to help sail a yacht from Melbourne to Opua, in the north part of the North Island of New Zealand. Coincidentally, as one of the first European settlements, the region was also the site of the first vineyards in New Zealand.

Although I was new to sailing and had done some time around in-shore bays, sailing had always made sense to me, especially the idea of sailing off, Mark Twain–like, 'away from the safe harbour to explore, dream, discover'. And on this trip, I figured, I might learn something more about the viticultural climate we know as 'maritime'.

I chose wines from maritime regions to drink on the yacht. Even more particularly, they were from Australian and New Zealand maritime regions – it was a Tasman crossing, after all. I chose sparkling from Tasmania, riesling from Margaret River, chardonnay from the Mornington Peninsula, rosé from McLaren Vale and pinot noir from Marlborough.

On the calm days we ate and drank at the table in the cockpit, like a floating dinner party, the parliament of our own country.

On the long stints between jobs or action, the ocean's greatness stretched the imagination to wonderment on a grand scale. I read once that you are more creative and inspired when you work in a large room. With no walls or ceiling to trim your thoughts, the ocean was that times a million.

Noting the clarity of water in such depths and surmising that, technically, that far out and that deep, humans had probably never touched it, we began to imagine the whole pristine world before mankind ever wandered it. 'Can you imagine?' Becoming conscious of its silent power and importance, we started to advocate for nature.

Other times, it was simple facts that had us in awe. 'Last night we crossed the continental shelf of Australia and went from two hundred to four thousand metres deep.' Of course, nothing

## THE TEMPERING EFFECT

The wine-growing regions of the world are classified into three broad climates that determine the styles of wines made and the varieties that can be grown well.

Maritime regions are those wine regions near the sea, including Bordeaux and much of New Zealand. They are defined by a more consistent year-round temperature, due to the moderating effect of the sea, and can often be subject to higher rainfall and humidity than other climates.

Continental regions are those inland regions, not near large bodies of water, that have a large difference between their highest and lowest temperatures, including regions such as Burgundy, Rioja, Mendoza and Piedmont.

Mediterranean climates are those that are generally warmer and drier than either the continental or maritime climates, and that maintain a warmer temperature throughout winter.

looked different, but we still all looked down in wonder.

We watched whales breech, had a visit from a shearwater bird who sailed with us for a night, woke to flying fish, baby squids and a lantern fish that had landed on deck and, as is the case on every yacht I have been on, ended up talking about the great adventurers and their journeys – Shackleton's South Pole epic, how Norwegian Roald Amundsen beat the Brit Robert Scott in a race to discover the South Pole (probably because Amundsen packed dogs instead of ponies), and Jack London's exploits on his dodgy ship the *Snark*.

On the heavy days, the idea of smelling a wine's nuance seemed utterly ridiculous. I understood why pirates and sailors drank hard spirits in swigs and slugs – it was the most return with the least spillage in that tiny break between swells, its potency fitting for such an event: like doing a shot with the wild ocean.

In viticulture, maritime regions are created because of the tempering effect of nearby oceans. Because the mass of water never freezes, it keeps the temperature higher and creates a more moderate climate. Inland continental regions, on the other hand, experience large extremes between day and night temperatures. That's the role of the ocean in maritime regions: it calibrates the extremes.

But sailing across the Tasman on that yacht, in the middle of the gale, I wondered how such monumental forces could temper anything, least of all a vineyard.

These were forces generated by the trade winds blowing in from the north, and the strong and cool southerlies generated below; both these weather patterns have a long fetch, ultimately clashing in the middle like two spinning tops turning in opposite directions.

After a few days, as if someone had turned off the gas on a stovetop, the boiling water simmered, then flattened. The gale passed, and we continued our journey more easily.

Later, back on land, when people asked how the trip was, it was always hard to explain. I could say I sailed, but it was more that I *endured* the Tasman Sea; I could say it was fun but it was more purposeful than fun; I could say it was an adventure, but it felt closer to an achievement. I could try to explain the power and awe of being part of the ocean for twelve days, but instead I re-told stories about breeching whales and heavy gales, as if that came anywhere close to explaining it.

Everyone asked if I was scared. I never was, though it's important to note I was never in charge either. I was extremely uncomfortable at times, and when that happened, I felt closer to something more thrilling than I have ever known, but every time I got through that, I felt more capable. I think along the way, I readjusted my levels. And that's when I finally got it: the ocean did to me what it does to numerous maritime wine regions the world over. It calibrated my extremes.

*'For whatever we lose (like a you or a me)*
*it's always ourselves we find in the sea.'*

—*e.e. cummings*

## MATCHING WINE

I 'm no relationship expert, but I have often wondered if we spend too much time trying to match or equal our partner's attributes, rather than complement them with wildly opposite traits. I can see the logic behind this idea of making a matching team: someone with less of whatever you have will somehow hold you back or dilute your virtues. Others explain it by saying they are just trying to align with someone with common goals.

But even though I can see the reason, I am not sure it's quite right. Sometimes people make better sense when complemented by someone different. Most of the happy relationships I see are when dysfunctions are matched. I think it's the wrong approach to look for someone who is faultless, rather than looking for someone who has tolerable faults; faults you might one day find delicious.

Food-and-wine matching is a bit like that; there are many rules and ideals, and some truly magnificent classic matches that will always be. But there are also some strange and unexpected matches made up of items that only find a home when paired with another; awkward loners who seem less than perfect on their own, but together create the famed 'third flavour', a bubble of gastronomical happiness when the two complement each other. Years ago, when philosophising about relationships, a wise friend suggested I list the top eight things I expected in a partner. Happy with my list, I handed it over. He said, 'Right, now pick three of them because that's all you'll get – and then make space for another five you would never imagine but will most certainly get.'

Food and wine matching is a bit like that: we can point to ideals and principles that work, but if you're adventurous, you might also get to delight in a few surprise matches. Even if it is just for dinner.

### ❦ TASTING NOTES ❦

❦ Try the classic matches: blue cheese and Sauternes, pinot noir and duck, lobster and chardonnay, riesling and grilled fish, champagne and oysters, lamb and cabernet sauvignon. Like iconic cities and great novels, they have endured for good reason.

❦ Experiment with new ideas: sweeter gewürztraminer and rieslings are gaining ground as fantastic matches with spicy Thai and Vietnamese dishes.

❦ Keep an open mind and a space at the table for the odd matches: a top sommelier recently told me of a surprise match between a sagrantino, one of the most tannic varieties in the world and one that usually takes decades to soften, and a piece of pork belly. The fat from the pork balanced out the usually antisocial acid and tannins. All about matching dysfunctions.

# MERLOT

❦ *Happy New Year!*' she chirped as I walked into the salon. It was actually a few days into the new year and, although the salon was quiet, she was humming and busy.

There was something different about her. A young woman, she seemed older, more engaged.

'How was it?' I asked, taking a seat at the basin.

'Oh my god ... it was seriously ... *the* best night of my life.'

I had known her ever since she came as an apprentice several years ago. When she first started out she was shy, handing foils, passing pins and folding towels as requested.

Over the years of appointments, I'd heard discussions about diets, how to hide bloating, underage drinking, and saw new boys come and go over text-message sagas.

Now she has her own business and, at half my age, she often seems twice as settled. She runs a house, has a dog and talks about 'settling down' as if there was more to settle.

I sometimes forget how young she is – until she confirms my appointment with a smiley face.

'It was amazing, so beautiful, the best New Year's – no, the best *night* ever,' she continued.

She had spoken of her plans for New Year's Eve – dinner and celebrations at a winery – for weeks in the lead up. She had a make-up practice run and a special dress fitting with the girl-friends she was going with.

'We had our photo taken with the most amazing backdrop. The sunset was so gorgeous.'

She was always lively and spoke of mischief and fun, but there was a new adoration in her descriptions.

## SMOOTH OPERATOR

Soft, succulent, smooth, silky, velvety, juicy merlot. The red wine famed for its 'smoothness', it is also this 'smoothness' that many see as the variety's weakness. Merlot grapes are naturally light on for acid and tannin, which makes the wine smooth and approachable right after release. When it's good, merlot brims with lovely berry aromas of raspberry and blackberry, through to plums, figs, prunes and spice.

I could imagine the setting on such an exquisite night. The yawning valley had been green and lush that summer. A hot summer day, with no wind or storm front to unsettle it – the night would have been magnificent, balmy and calm until well after the sun went down on the year.

As she did my hair, we discussed the food: the entrees, the mains and gorgeous desserts.

'But the wine,' she said, 'I have never tasted anything like it.'

I watched her in the mirror in front of us. This was the first time we'd spoken of wine in this way. 'What was it?' I asked.

'I don't remember, I just asked them for a smooth red,' she said sweetly, yet holding her chin a little higher. I wonder if it was a merlot – a famously smooth red wine, soft and supple with no pointy edges.

'The wine was just so beautiful. It was amazing. I even bought a bottle to take away. I wanted to sip it on the way home in the car, but I just held it on my lap and saved it.'

I asked her which winery, but she couldn't remember that either. Started with a 'B' maybe?

'How should I look after it? I've wrapped it up in a towel and put it in my bedroom cupboard for now.'

I offered some temporary cellaring advice. Though, as ever, she was looking after things well already.

She explained that she and her boyfriend had an important dinner with his father, and she wanted to bring the wine. 'His dad is the only person I know who is into wine.'

I was curious at her new fondness: it literally happened overnight.

'It sounds like you had a great night,' I said. She smiled and laughed occasionally as scenes flashed by and she retold more stories.

'Do you think I can buy more of the wine?' she asked as I was leaving. I made some suggestions on how she might, without knowing the name of the winery, but deep down I wondered if her next bottle of the same wine could ever be as good – or if, in fact, any bottle of wine would ever be as special.

## MINDFULNESS

Hemingway, in his novel *The Sun Also Rises*, alluded to the importance of a clear mind when it comes to enjoying wine: a type of wine mindfulness, if you like. A busy mind, whether preoccupied by too much emotion or a hectic day, distracts from how we taste, sense and perceive wine. To have a head full of noise while trying to note the aromatic subtleties, structural shifts or the textural nuances of a wine is like going to the orchestra and

### WINE MEDITATION

Sometimes, when tasting wine, I momentarily close my eyes while thinking about it. I know, it seems a little intense but it helps by cutting out the distractions, like a little mini-meditation on the wine. And in that moment when you do close your eyes, you sort of go somewhere else – which is a nice way to think about the wine and, depending on where you are, can be a nice thing, too.

trying to read while a hundred musicians perform Beethoven's Fifth. How can you hear anything but the opening four chords? How will you ever get the hidden themes, the string harmonies or the synergies created from them all? Enjoying wine is the same. If you want to hear what the wine has to say, quiet your mind, then listen.

*'This wine is too good for toast-drinking, my dear. You don't want to mix emotions up with a wine like that. You lose the taste.'*

—*Ernest Hemingway*, The Sun Also Rises

## MOSCATO

Moscato is where sparkling wine gets cute, quirky and refreshing. Though slightly *frizzante*, moscato is happy to leave the high-stakes glamour events to the world's most famous bubbles and her followers – to the ladies who stride effortlessly, heads held high, oozing confidence, breathing charm, with lips trimmed in a red as vivid as the soles of their four-inch Louboutins.

Moscato's not that girl and she knows it. She's the girl you wouldn't call glamorous, but you would call super stylish. Who doesn't do 'fashion', but quietly shines in vintage couture. Who's less about sultry seduction and more about enchanting with sweetness and charm. Moscato is something all picnic hampers, long lunches and cheeky brunches should have. Think pancakes, fruit, ice-cream, a gingham cloth and a sunny afternoon.

But isn't this old fashioned? A bit simple? Didn't my grandma used to drink this? Sure, but your grandma also took lovers in Italy and smoked in jazz bars before you knew how to tie your rollerskates.

Serve chilled with a genuine smile and a lick of gloss.

## 🍇 Tasting notes 🍇

🍇 Moscato gained fresh legs when the rest of the winemaking world spent a bit of time in Italy and realised that the sweet, bubbly drop that's lower in alcohol, with a cheeky pink blush, is as simple and sweet as it looks.

🍇 We are currently in the middle of a moscato wave of popularity; older winemakers who saw it go out are still scratching their heads and kicking the dirt, wondering how this happened, and those who always liked their wine a little sweet with a kick of spritz can't believe their luck.

# MUSIC

After food and conversation, and perhaps one or two other more private things, I suspect music has been accompanying and contributing to the enjoyment of wine forever – and I imagine it will continue to do so for a long time to come.

Intuitively we know that listening to music while drinking wine makes things better. Some claim that the type, speed and loudness of music affects how much pleasure you taste. The louder and faster the music, the faster you drink and the more robust things taste.

So if this is what music does to us, what does it do to the plants? Many have heard of stories about the wacky vigneron who played music to his vines and to his wines in the barrel hall, in the hope of soothing them and helping them grow or age gracefully. Nice guy, wrong planet? Maybe not.

## 'In music the passions enjoy themselves.'

—*Friedrich Nietzsche*

Many winemakers believe the vibrations caused by excess handling, working or use of machinery damages the grapes, so surely the reverse would also be true: playing symphonies in the vineyards would enhance them.

Let's look at it another way. The most important mantra in meditation is a vibration. It symbolises the belief that absolutely everything in the universe is in a state of vibration – thoughts, matter, material – everything. It is chanted roughly a jillion times a day and has been for centuries. It is said to calm the mind and heal the sick. It is of course, the Om, the 'vibration of the supreme'.

No matter which way you look at it, music, mellifluous vibration, whether for you or the vines, is important. Choose your tracks wisely.

## TASTING TO THE MUSIC

In-store music selections can affect your buyer behaviour, so it's no surprise that music – the type, tempo, pace, volume and style – can also affect your wine-buying and drinking choices. According to some studies, the faster the pace of the music, the faster you drink. Another shows that the type of music can affect what you think you taste in wine. In one study, people imagined the same qualities they found in the music – powerful and heavy or bright and boppy – in the wines they drank. So, if you feel your guest complains that the cabernet is a little too dark and broody, rather than open another bottle, perhaps spin some Kylie to give it a little lift.

# MYSTERY

I was standing with a group of wine-interested people in a corrugated iron shed set high amongst some McLaren Vale vineyards. On the table in front of us was a very particular set of things: various plastic bags of mixtures and emulsions, jars we weren't allowed to open, clumps of dirt and old cow horns.

We were being shown how biodynamics, the method of farming

created by Austrian philosopher Rudolf Steiner, works. Our guide was explaining the controversial process of making the preparations 500 and 501. To make these preparations, you stuff cow horns with manure or quartz, then bury and leave them for a season, after which you mix the stuffings with water and spray it on the vineyards. 'We really don't know why it makes the vineyards react so well, but it does.'

Fascinating.

Someone chuckled.

Another couple rolled their eyes at each other.

I'll admit, it did sound a little potion-like, but it also sounded quite exciting in the way that wonders of the world are quite enticing. It occurred to me how, if we dismissed everything we couldn't explain in life but knew to be true, we'd live in a much smaller and less hopeful world.

Over years of talking with winemakers, one of the things that strikes me is how often they say, 'We don't actually know.' Whether it's in the winemaking stages in the vineyard, the winery or the cellar, wine is infused with mysteries that even the most experienced find hard to explain.

For example, when it comes to bottles ageing, there are many scientific processes that occur that explain some of what happens – but not all of it. Like why one bottle ages differently to the same bottle lying right next to it. Another winemaker, walking me through a vintage and showing me the warm, bubbling fermenting cap of skins, said they don't really know what happens under the cap of the fermenting wine. They know the science, but not what accounts for all of the variations and nuances of the resulting wine from one ferment to the next.

In the vineyard, things are just as mysterious. Establishing which varieties and clones do well is a combination of art, science and, as some winemakers profess, a bit of mystery. One winemaker once said to me, 'We know each site produces wines of different personalities. Some clones do well on some sites in some years, some do better in others. But we don't always know why and we don't pretend to know.'

I love this mystery in wine, not least because it adds to the wonder and uniqueness of our experience. I mean, who doesn't like a drink that can make you wonder and make you think, but also gives permission to believe in a lot of other, more private, hopes and joys?

## MYSTERIOUS PREPARATIONS

Biodynamic agriculture relies on nine preparations that are based on plant, mineral and animal substances and are all aimed at helping fertilisation. They are numbered from 500 to 508. Preparation 500 is basically fermented cow manure, and 501 is ground quartz. The first preparation is achieved by stuffing a cow horn with manure and burying it underground for the winter. Upon retrieval a small amount of the fermented manure is mixed into a bucket of water and stirred – both ways – for an hour before being sprayed on the vineyard to improve soil and microbiological health. Preparation 501 is made by a similar means, except the horn is stuffed with ground quartz over summer and the resultant mixture is sprayed over the vines instead of vineyards.

Because if we can believe that something magical is happening in nature, despite us or our limited knowledge, we can also believe in anything else we want to from the universe: that the one you have been waiting for is just around the corner; that if there is no cure, there might soon be one; that just because it hasn't doesn't mean it can't.

So when someone, winemaker or other, says they know

something happens but they can't explain why it does, believe them … and then keep believing in absolutely anything and everything else you want to.

*'The most beautiful thing we can experience is the mysterious. It is the source of all true art and science.'*

—*Albert Einstein*

## NARRATIVE

When you think about it, it's hard to know where a wine's story really begins.

Despite the information provided on a label, a wine's narrative doesn't really start at its first vintage. It doesn't even start when it was first bottled, or when the grapes were first picked, or even when the vines were first planted.

In fact, I am not even sure a wine's narrative has a beginning or end; rather, it is more like a complex amalgam of ongoing narratives, sometimes spanning centuries, covering politics and religion, philosophy and science, nature and geology, fused together in a wonderful and lovely drink. This is another of the remarkable things about wine: there is little it doesn't engage with.

I sometimes imagine, when a bottle is opened and the wine poured, that these narratives are released to unwind like climbing vines, weaving their way into the lives of others; keeping the stories alive while the source of them continues to be elsewhere.

The idea of narratives – of where they begin and end – dawned on me recently when I went to an event where families came together after many years apart. For reasons I am still trying to understand, and through no singular event or reason, I had not seen many of them for a very long time. But stepping back in I realised you can't just pick up where you left off. We, too, carry a series of narratives within us, many of which involve us and keep developing even when we are not present.

For some people, such inherited tales are a wonderful story on which to enter life, placing them immediately in a position and context of interestingness and privilege. But for others, inherited stories can be as star-crossed as the family background of Shakespeare's famous lovers.

Like a human being, wine is a vector for the tales that came before it, the ones it inhabits, and those it creates on its own, given the chance.

Some wines tell a geological story by expressing the earth they spring from, such as those of Heathcote, grown in the ancient Precambrian soils – not only do they reflect particular viticultural expressions, but also the ancientness of the Australian continent.

A wine might also harbour a religious story, as do those of Burgundy, which were heavily influenced by the Cistercian monks, who were some of the first to notice that certain sites consistently expressed unique characteristics, thus germinating the concept of terroir and the complex crus or classified growths of Burgundy.

Other wines tell political narratives, such as those from Greece, which are currently undergoing a new start after much of their ancient wine history lay dormant under the rule of the Ottoman Empire.

All wines, literally or mythologically, historically or scientifically, reflect a particular cluster of narratives.

Over the years, many of us engaged with wine have described its bottling as capturing a moment in time – like momentarily freezing the dynamic process of winemaking. But as I understand both wine and life a little bit more, I am not so sure this is accurate. I've come to think a bottle of wine as less about an isolated moment in time and more like a vessel that has been dipped into, and filled from, the stream that is the flowing continuum of life.

## NATURE'S OFFERINGS

A s I was learning of the varying and terrifying heats of chillies, I came to the conclusion that nature gives us just the right size of her fruits and wares that we can handle. The more petite the chilli, the fiercer and more ferocious the heat – so much so, you might think the tiny red ones look just like an infant devil's horns, plucked shiny and fiery straight from his menacing little head. Eat one of those scaled up to the size of a banana and you might die.

When I applied my hypothesis, a kind of theory of natural perfection (however misguided), to various fruits and vegetables in my life at the time, it seemed to hold true. Apples: quite

## QUALITY AND QUANTITY

Generally speaking, it is thought that the lower the yield, the better the quality of wine, for the reasons explained here.

Lower yields are achieved by crop thinning or shoot thinning. However, a low yield alone is no guarantee of better quality wine, particularly as low yields can also come about from poor conditions – in which case the resulting fruit might be low in quantity, but also of inferior quality.

a perfect-sized snack, and harmless and handy enough to eat a second. Oranges: a rewarding and gorgeous activity for one, with all that unwrapping and separating ensuring you'll only stick to one dose of sugar.

The bulbous universe that is the watermelon might have proved me wrong, until I recalled hot summer days spent with friends as a child, handling an arc of watermelon large enough to hold a rocking horse, and realised that watermelons grow that large because they are supposed to be a communal eating experience. Can you imagine eating a slice of watermelon alone?

Of course this theory of natural perfection doesn't always work; I mean, what of a pumpkin? Or a cherry?

As unscientific as it might be, it can be a useful – albeit loose – guide to eating. When so many portion sizes are no longer controlled by nature, it's easy to lose sight of how much of anything to eat. Marketers, wishing to manipulate eating behaviour for company return, have created more eating occasions than we ever had and more sizes than we'll ever need: packets, snacks, on-the-go, jumbo, between meals, man size and fun size. What happened to natural size?

When it comes to wine, messages around the perfect serve aren't so straightforward either. Right now, you could probably find advice telling you not to drink, to drink between one and infinity glasses a day, that drinking gives you cancer, that it doesn't, that it might, but not if you're French because then none of this applies to you.

Thinking about this size hypothesis, this theory of natural perfection, as it applies to wine, I wondered what portion of wine nature thought was best for us. A grape? A bunch? A vine? A hill? Well, let's work this out. An average-ish vine growing up in a viticulturally perfect world will have around twenty shoots on it, give or take. Each of these shoots produces one bunch of grapes. One bunch of grapes is about 100 grams, and it takes about ten bunches of grapes to make one bottle, so each vine makes about two bottles of wine.

That's all well and good, except vines in their natural state look nothing like the groomed, trimmed and manicured plants we see in modern vineyards. In its wild and natural state, a grapevine is a wild and tangly climber.

To get it to a tidy, well-behaved vine, we trim and prune, train and trellis the vine to suit our needs. The two-bottles-to-a-vine idea is a modern idea, *our* idea, not really what nature gave us at all.

So, just as I am happy to take nature's suggestion on serving sizes when it comes to apples and watermelons and things like that, I am just as happy to take her suggestion for how much wine is a fair and reasonable amount. Because what nature gave us is much more generous than two bottles ... what she gave us is boundless.

'All good things are wild and free.'

—Henry David Thoreau

## NATURE'S TRICKS

The more I think about it, the more of a genius nature is. If you look around the world and take in all the different terrains, and all the by-products of these terrains, nature has created a slew of unique and particular treats for us to draw pleasure from.

Flowers alone are a joy enough, especially when you consider the variety, colour, depth, detail and brilliance that these precious little masterpieces provide, even when somewhere between life and death in a vase on the table. As Iris Murdoch said, 'People from a planet without flowers would think we must be mad with joy the whole time to have such things about us.'

Waves, those lovely and powerful expressions of energy from deep below, are another fun-park trick from nature, lifting people up and throwing them around, drawing people off the beaches, away from the cities, out of their suits and uniforms to play and frolic in the ocean's frills. And then, twice a day, as she pulls back the curtain to give beachcombers a look at what lies beneath, she draws us even further into the wonder and possibilities of the ocean and her abyss.

Hills are another joy – whether it's for the view from the top or the ride and slide down them when they're covered in snow. They offer much in the way of natural pleasures.

And of course there is wine, perhaps one of nature's most generous and pleasurable offerings. Whether for your gastronomical, romantic or other such pleasure, if nature could have created one thing to ensure we stay engaged with it, surely this is it.

Some say that to believe nature is here for our benefit is a tad conceited – or to think that some larger organising force is at work is plain crazy.

Whether these tricks are good design, good fortune or wishful thinking, I still think it's a wonderful trick because, as well as creating joy for many the world over, nature is also creating groups of dedicated fans – people who hopefully will advocate for it, give a little back, for what they have been given.

## NERO D'AVOLA

It was the first time I had been to the bar, and it was as cosy as everyone said it would be – a lounge room for locals. When they speak of this bar, they do it in the kind of clubby 'how could you not know' way. It was a long narrow room lit with soft lights, with a wooden bar, which ran the length of the room, featuring gaping silver wine buckets filled with opened wines. Behind the bar, a

## THE BLACK GRAPE OF AVOLA

Stark landscapes, rugged coastlines, an active volcano and an infamous culture layered with darkness and spice. If you had to guess what the 'black grape of Avola' in Sicily tastes like, you would pretty much land on the pleasures of nero d'Avola, Sicily's most important red grape: a heady blend of spice, savouriness, dried herbs, depth and dark berries. Given nero d'Avola's ability to work hard in hot and arid areas, expect and welcome versions of this variety from other similar climates such as South Australia.

sliding wooden ladder serviced a wall of high shelves brimming with imported wine and spirits.

The seats at the bar were almost full when we arrived, and we had to shuffle another couple up to take the last two seats. Everyone appeared intimately engaged with a close partner or friend. Couples sat close and faced each other, touching, conversations focused and not distracted. I couldn't believe it had taken us so long to visit, and I was, I admit, slightly envious of the intimacy that everyone appeared to share with the place.

We chose a glass of the Sicilian variety nero d'Avola to go with our platter of cold cuts, anchovies, bread and olives. This is a red wine deep and rich in colour, and with savoury and red berry flavours.

Over a few drinks, we noticed small signs that we too were becoming part of the community: the barman filling our glasses with more Italian wine because he knew that to be our preference; when someone at the bar ordered cold cuts, we knew to clear a part of the bar for the meat slicer's back-and-forth movements; and when the waiter was busy, we could re-tell quirks of the menu the waiter had shared with us to new customers. We became part of the locals' lounge room.

The bar and the room filled, the red wine warmed our insides and the atmosphere of the room opened us up. Our conversations became more intimate as we sat and drank closely. People bumped us from behind as they waited for a place at the bar. The barman opened the second bottle of nero d'Avola for us. It was oxidised. 'See?' he said, while we all tried a glass and waited for the bitterness on the palate that comes from oxidised wine, looking at each other in our small huddle, nodding and noticing the effect as we did.

A woman walked into the bar, dark hair and red lips, very that side of town. The barman left his post to greet her and kissed her on both cheeks. My feeling of being in a clique evaporated – I suddenly felt out of place. As she was bumped by others moving around the room, she lamented how she couldn't get a table.

I signalled that we would go soon, but the barman said no it's fine, enjoy, did we want a glass of grappa? I felt pleased that we had been prioritised, then suddenly foolish and petty for thinking such a thing.

It reminded me of the shallow and fleeting bite you get when people look like they're having more fun than you on Facebook. But at least in real life we had something literal to savour.

'Yes,' I said, relaxing back into my position at the bar, 'Two glasses of grappa.'

## OCCASIONS

I opened a beautiful bottle of perfumed and seductive pinot noir, and poured glasses large enough to signal this was going to be our whole night. He commented on how beautiful the wine was – whatever this wine had to say, it was something he heard.

It was a warm and still night toward the end of the season, when the warmth was gentle and felt more like autumn than the heat of summer.

The inner-city neighbourhood, which was often quite noisy, hummed with quiet notes and gentle conversations, as though the whole block had softened for a casual evening in.

The opening piano notes from Tom Waits' 'closing time' tinkled out from the house while we prepared to cook our dinner.

We ate our meal outside: a grilled fillet steak with a large mush-room, shiny and smooth with melted butter, and a few salad leaves picked from the small vegetable garden.

As the tunes wafted through the open door, we sipped our wine and spoke of things in the future. He took a photo as I held a glass and smiled.

We touched feet under the table and sipped the wine that helped to infuse the night with beauty.

It was a perfect match for the occasion, although those more specialised might actually say the meal called for something more robust. But would we have had the same night with another wine? Had we opened an intense cabernet sauvignon – with its dark fruit and cedar notes, its earnest and ordered palate – we may have had a different conversation. Or what if one of us had demanded a white wine with energising acid? I wonder, would it have been the same?

## IDEAL WINE OCCASIONS

As well as having the ability to pair with many particular ingredients, many wines are capable of setting a tone regardless of the food: a rosé gives a nod to beautifully casual moments; nothing says a mini-celebration more than a glass of champagne; pinot noir, of course, and many say the great nebbiolos, have a seductive perfume and layers of complexity to help you engage with wonderful food and an intellectual curiosity. And cabernet sauvignon, with its structure and dark berries, like a frown and a pinstripe – if you want a wine to complement such a moment, the king might well be your partner.

Of course there are wine and food matches capable of making the elusive third flavour. But, as beautiful as these can be, I've often wondered if wine-and-food matching would benefit from being matched to the occasion – or what we would like the occasion to be – rather than to the minutiae of a dish.

*'Sharing food with another human being is an intimate act that should not be indulged in lightly.'*

—*M.F.K. Fisher*

## OLD WORLD, NEW WORLD

The 'Old World' and 'New World' labels in winemaking refer as much to regions and countries as to approaches to winemaking. Many say they are outdated generalisations, too broad to be meaningful indicators of anything more than geography, while others say there are certain characteristics that are largely typical of the two regions.

Perhaps these distinctions were more fitting in the past: back when the new wine world was starting out and the Old World was much more experienced.

It reminds me of the discussion around birth order in families, which some argue is a predictor of personality. The theory goes that the oldest kids are the most conservative, the middle are ignored and the last spend their lives rebelling against the dominance of those that went before them. For these last children it's like turning up late to a party when the seats are full, conversations are under way, bonds are formed and roles are already assigned; so they rebel against this order and carve out their own unique path. Maybe the New World styles were an attempt to do everything the Old World couldn't?

Today, to say a New World or Old World style of wine exists is no more accurate than saying a New World or Old World style of person exists. These days worlds are merging, and some even say civilisations don't so much exist geographically but *virtually*, as traditional borders are usurped for technological ones.

In recent years both 'worlds' have benefited by borrowing from each other's pool of talents. There are many excellent examples of wineries in New World regions making wines in traditional, terroir-driven styles, and of Old World countries utilising technology to make more international styles of wine. And the reverse is true in both regions as well.

Of course, quality wine – by law and design – will always be tied to geographic areas, some with more particular detail than others. Wine will always need to be *from* somewhere. Maybe this is one of the beautiful truths about wine: that when the world merges and distinctions between cultures are blurred, the only thing left that is truly unique is the patch of land it's grown from.

For now, I think these definitions help us to understand the context of recent developments and how these wine 'civilisations' shaped the world of wine we know today. But we should keep in mind that the younger siblings, though they'll always be younger, are not children anymore.

## ❦   TASTING NOTES   ❦

❦   The Old World winemaking regions include countries such
as Italy, France, Spain and Germany.

❦   New World countries include America, Australia, New
Zealand, Chile, Argentina and South Africa.

❦   While the Old World was largely about traditional
techniques and an artisanal approach to winemaking, the New
World benefitted from technology that helped to control the
winemaking process.

❦   In the past, New World wines relied on showcasing varieties
and brands; Old World wineries focused on wines that were an
expression of place.

❦   New World wines were fruit driven and approachable on
release, while Old World ones were subtle, savoury and often
needed time to develop.

❦   Today, to say entire 'worlds' produce wine in the same style
is an outdated view. Similarities may well exist in winemakers'
philosophies or approaches to winemaking, but these are defined
by their philosophies and approaches to winemaking, not by
which 'world' their country of origin was once classified in.

## ORDERING FROM A WINE LIST

I get it a lot, the wine list. I think this is completely understand-able, though I used to think it was because I write about wine when in fact I suspect it's because I am writing a book. These days, wine lists look like a book: the sheets, the layers, the weight, the names and sections that go on and on.

But despite the intimidating and biblical weight of many lists, there is order to them. And when you understand them, it can be liberating when you know how easy they are to navigate. It's like finally seeing the image on those 3D puzzles – you'll welcome the next one that lands on your lap.

Generally, wines on wine lists are written in order from light to heavy, in white and then red. But before all of those come the fun stuff – cocktails, aperitifs and sparkling wines – and at the end of the list come the digestifs and fortified wines – the super-heavy stuff.

Remember those lucky kids at school who had a set of seventy-two Derwent pencils? Lined up properly, they were like an ordered kaleidoscope of colour. And remember how you could get about ten different shades of, say, yellow and just as many shades of red? That's what we mean by weight. A wine list works a bit like that. All the whites – light to heavy followed by all the reds, light to heavy.

Once you know how the list is ordered, here are some things you should consider to continue narrowing down your options: What are you eating? What's the occasion? What do *you* like? Who are you dining with?

Another thing to note is that, just like with 3D puzzles, it's easy to lose focus with a wine list. When this happens, always feel welcome to ask the waiter or sommelier. They are a wonderful and knowledgeable source of information, and a turnkey to unlock so many new and interesting wines from around the world.

## ❦ TASTING NOTES ❦

TIPS ON NARROWING DOWN YOUR WINE LIST SELECTION:

❦ *What's the occasion?* Some occasions are more special than others and call for more special wines, while others just require a perfect match for pizza. Of course, what you deem to be special is personal and might include something more expensive, aged, imported, or something that's super boutique. There are ideal wines for all occasions.

❦ *Are you after a light, medium or full-bodied wine?* In white wine you can get a whole range of weights, as you can in red wine. These varying weights are dependent on the variety (some are naturally heavier than others) and also on how it's made (some techniques make wines heavier or richer than others). Most good wine lists are ordered like this, in both red and white wines. You just need to work out where you sit on the scale.

❦ *What weight of food are you eating?* Both your food and your wine have a better chance of shining when paired with something of equal weight. So once you have pegged your moment and your weight preferences, try a general food match.

❦ *Who are you dining with?* You see, even within these parameters, there are still options. I know some people who just don't like certain varieties and others who, when they drink a red, like to feel a little weight in their wine. So try to include a wine that suits your companion's preferences as well, which changes depending on who you dine with.

## PACKAGING PUFFERY

Wineries rely on packaging to communicate the wine's position and noteworthy information to potential buyers. The armoury of tools involved in packaging includes the bottle weight, back and front labels, medal stickers and writing about the winery, its philosophy, background or pedigree. These, together, are designed to project an intended position and image – sometimes, one that is even aligned with the quality of the wine.

When it *isn't* matched to what's inside, it reminds me of the kind of person who uses a particular suite of words, clothing and behaviours to project a certain image that is disconnected from what's inside. For some of these types of people, there's always the tone that implies they are so important they have a direct message for God, no matter who is on the other line, a local pizza delivery guy or taxi despatcher: 'Hello, Ben is it?' Pause. 'Robert Tyler Hudson here.' It's not necessarily the name that gets poor Ben, it's the pause that implies, 'I'll give you a moment to get my file.' Ben now turns every cell to Robert, just in case, at which this man continues, 'Tell me Ben, do you have ...'

*'Noise proves nothing. Often a hen who has merely laid an egg cackles as if she had laid an asteroid.'*

—Mark Twain

That's another thing – they always use the person's name in a way that says, 'I've got your number, and I'm not afraid to call your mum.'

Just like making your bottles as heavy as possible or plastering them with gold-medal stickers, money – and inferring the possession of a lot of it – is also a common bit of puffery. But only if referred to in passing, as though they have so much of it that it's like a secondary and hilarious inconvenience: 'Oh, I had the car serviced this week. Those Germans! One timing belt on that thing is $11,000. I can't believe the wife talked me into getting her the top-of-the-range model – again!'

Not to say that such things can *never* equate to quality – of course they sometimes do, otherwise imitators wouldn't bother emulating and borrowing. And not to say that such livery doesn't look good or even make us feel good. But with wine, as with life, it's not enough on its own – because it's what's on the inside that really determines one's worth.

## ❦  TASTING NOTES  ❦

❦  Bottle weight is often used to signal a higher quality wine. These days, many wineries are looking at lighter weight bottles to minimise their carbon footprint. But no matter how thick the glass on a standard bottle, it's still 750 mls.

❦  Mostly, titles such as 'premium selection', 'family reserve' and 'cellar selection' allude to nothing more than names given to different tiers of their wine portfolio.

❦  Putting stickers of medals on wine bottles does appeal to many consumers, but before you buy a wine based on the medals that adorn it, check what the competition was, and whether the award is in fact for that wine.

# PINOT NOIR

*'Dear Kate, I'm sorry. I wish I could be there to help. We could go for some Peking duck and pinot noir and you could tell me all about it.'*

It was as much comfort as I could give in a letter to someone so far away. My friend in London was separating from her husband of ten years.

## THE SIREN OF WINES

No wine variety captivates quite like pinot noir. A red wine archetype of such beauty, sensuality and allure, she attracts admirers with her perfume and complexity and bewitches them for life. Pinot noir is the reason many are enchanted with wine and, like an expert seductress, she is inconsistent in her rewards, which only seems to make the fascination stronger. For winemakers, pinot noir is a challenge to make but a joy to master; fickle at every stage and easy to leave fingerprints on, she is tempestuous to the end. When pinot noir is good, she expresses sensuousness, layers and alluring perfume; when she is bad, she's *Betty Blue*.

I met Kate seven years ago at business school, where we bonded quickly over partying, shared opinions and food. She always seemed more single than married, in the way that single people are spontaneous, spirited and have full access to their own diaries. Since then she has roamed the world until she finds a city charged enough to take her on, then she dives in and rolls around in it like a baby in a bath. When it teaches her something new, changes her a bit, gives her something to think about or just starts to look familiar, she moves on. This gusto for the new makes her an adventurous friend and even better dining partner ... if you can catch her.

Aside from watery function meals between classes, our first meal together was at a Chinese restaurant we discovered that we both bowed to for its lo-fi interior, quality cuisine and underground foodie credentials that we both knew but didn't admit to. It was a culinary 'snap!' that connected us. Ten days together on a study program in Shanghai only cemented our connection. We ate our way around that wild city, taking risks, sharing plates, helping feed and explore each other's appetites.

So 'some Peking duck and pinot?' was an invitation to a tradition as savoured as Christmas.

It occurred to me just how many of my relationships were born on food and wine pairings that have defined and nourished the friendships over years.

Tracy was the first friend I shared a dining ritual with. We dined at a pasta joint in Chapel Street back when visiting stars still flocked to the strip. We made two bowls of gnocchi Alfredo – dissolving puffs of pasta knuckles covered in cream, bacon and shallots – fluffy white bread and carafes of house wine last for hours and hours. Lucky the waiters thought us cute. Six years ago she had a baby and, for some reason that escapes me now but was important to us both at the time, we stopped talking. I emailed recently, opening with 'Long time no gnocchi'. We have since eaten together often.

With Christine, when we regroup it's over a bowl of Vietnamese pho or Mexican – once upon a time she was the only other person I knew in Melbourne who thought Mexican was a legitimate cuisine that didn't need a hangover to justify it. Jack and I enjoy a steak from a gentrified Port Melbourne pub with a monster South Australian shiraz and a 'few off the wood' while we wonder where Maple the bar fly and the XP bookie have been relocated to; Amelia, a mother of four who cherishes her free time and good food, won't eat seafood for main, so requires premium meat, good red wine, and sincere service. Anne is particular and needs planning, but when she is there she devours food with such grace and pleasure it's sometimes distracting. She can be led on wine choices and is generous in what she is prepared to pay for good food – just don't rush her.

They're not all old rituals, either. Chris and I are just starting a tradition of a twelve-hour lamb dish and a hearty bottle of red from an inner-city eatery. He emailed recently, having had his first

child this year, 'Nearly ready for some lamb and a bottle of red.'
That'll be the third time; I guess this makes it tradition.

I'm not sure if these are my friends, and so we eat, or if they
are my friends *because* we eat. I suspect the latter. I have little time
for those who put a penny-pinching mood on what I can order at
dinner ... 'Let's just get one dish and if we're still hungry at the
end we can get another.' Or, 'You eat, I had something before I
got here.' Or, the death knell: 'Eating is cheating.' What do these
people *love*?

A good dining partner is precious and rare and, in the right
relationship, it seems impossible, even disloyal, to enjoy certain
dishes without them. Why some of these relationships form and
others don't is mysterious, precious and unique. A lid for every pot,
they say.

Good dining partners should also be good listeners, and selfless
enough to dedicate whole dinners to you. A bridesmaid to your
woe ... or win ... whatever the case may be.

If Kate were in town and not in London, this would be one of
those times. We'd go to our favourite restaurant for her. I would
go with a bottle of pinot noir, something good if I had any. I might
even start with a riesling or maybe a bottle of chardonnay. The
moment we'd walk in, the smells of roasted meats – star anise,
plums, sweet sticky coatings – would comfort and distract.

I would make them seat us on the side, against a wall, and not in
the middle, where we would be vulnerable to other people's ears.
The bright lights and open room already reveal enough. Until we
were ready, I'd shepherd the waiters away with my eyes and not let
them near if she was saying something hard.

I imagine she'd be overwhelmed, and so I would order for us, without looking at the menu: two bowls of seafood and bean-curd soup; a deep-fried quail in chilli and garlic; half a Peking duck; fish with ginger and shallots, or stir-fried beef with fried crispy egg noodles replacing the sloppy rice ones to give it more structure. Either wine would go – besides, there aren't really courses here, just a food rush until the end.

If we really felt like sitting in for a night, we'd go a mud crab with ginger and shallots, swimming in the tank until we ordered it. We'd roll up our sleeves, and talk and gnaw and suck the meat out of the claws and drink and get messy. Maybe the clumsiness of eating the crab would lighten her mood. I'd also get some special fried rice, even though the host would say it was too much because we already had the noodles with the crab. I'd order it anyway.

Over time, getting stuff off her chest and getting the good food and wine in, she would relax. We might laugh about something absurd – that we were sitting there eating enough for ten men, or that time she straddled the fake polar bear on display in the hotel lobby in Shanghai – and I'd hope she would feel better.

The thought of it makes me go to the restaurant one lunch-time, alone, ordering a simple clean serve of stir-fried fish and ginger and a pot of tea. As I am eating, I think of Kate and wonder how she is going, if she is sad in London in February. I decide to write her a letter. At the table I start …

*'Dear Kate, I'm so sorry. I wish I could be there to help. We could go for some Peking duck and pinot noir and you could tell me all about it.'*

## PRICE - *THE GREAT SWITCHEROO*

There are a few themes in the stories told about wine that non-wine people really latch on to.

One is the story that comes out in the news at least once a year that implies that wine writers and judges, when tested properly, can't tell one wine from another. The papers run stories that infer the whole system of assessing and enjoying wine is a joke: a culture with credibility levels somewhere between balance-bracelet ambassadors and Scientologists.

The comments sections run away with it:

'Hallelujah! Someone's finally told the emperor he's not wearing any clothes.'

'I've got one word to say: snake oil!'

One popular story tells of people who, when given the same wine in two glasses but told one is more expensive than the other, write better tasting notes and derive much greater pleasure from the more expensive wine.

'I knew it – pretentious jokers!'

In defence of wine, some say this is not a fault of wine connoisseurship at all, but more about society and how it values money. It's hardly the fault of the wine writer if you're the one who automatically thinks that something more expensive is better. Have you no capacity to judge something based on its merits? How shallow of you. The fault is not with wine, but with your skewed and superficial values.

It reminds me of a short story by Roald Dahl called *The Great Switcheroo*. This is one of Dahl's adult short stories that are wicked and naughty and layered with subtleties, twists and cunning.

Which is hardly surprising – even as a child, you knew there was something else super-clever going on in *Charlie and the Chocolate Factory*; Dahl was ten twists ahead of anyone, and these adult short stories just prove it.

*The Great Switcheroo*, which first appeared in *Playboy* magazine in the 70s, is about two men who are husbands, neighbours and close friends, who scheme to have sex with each other's wives without the wives knowing. They rely on the belief that the wives won't know the difference – that, and a kind of twisted moral compass.

In the story, the two men go about planning, plotting and scheming.

Things happen, and there's a twist.

I read the story again recently and it occurred to me, in a reve-latory two-handed face-slap way, that there might be more than one twist in this story, after all.

Some years ago I started seeing a man and, soon after we had realised that neither of us was embarrassed by each other in public, we went away with another couple for a weekend. Among all the 'are they a keeper, ha ha?' topics, we were talking about authors and I brought up Dahl's *The Great Switcheroo*.

Yes, this does get awkward.

I told the story because I was taken by Dahl's storytelling skills: undeniably brilliant. The conversation lingered on *The Great Switcheroo*, more than it had when I told it to anyone else.

'I'm sorry, I don't know,' I said as they started asking questions, turning my head from one side of the room and back to answer them all. 'What did they have on? He didn't really say,' … 'Music? No, um, I don't think there was any.'

They seemed so interested in the story, so on and on I went

about how funny and naughty it was that these two men SWAPPED WIVES.

I know, I can barely write it.

The worst bit, about *my* story, not Dahl's, is that I was presenting it just like Vic, the initiator of the idea in the actual story; he uses a made-up story to pitch the idea to his neighbour Jerry. In the kind of 'You won't believe what a friend of mine did' way, dangling the big bad carrot.

To people such as Jerry, my story was practically code for 'Ready when you are'. I might as well have tossed the salad out of the bowl, put my keys in and undressed there and then.

As I said, it's only now that it occurred to me that this might be Dahl's final trick with that story, that every time someone tells it, he starts the cycle again.

Or does he?

Which is sort of why all these wine-trick stories remind me of *The Great Switcheroo;* not because it's hard to know if the whole system is real or a trick, but whether, if there *is* a joke, the joke on us for writing it and believing what we write. Or is the joke on readers for reading what we write and believing it?

I guess we'll never know.

Or will we?

## ❦ TASTING NOTES ❦

### IS PRICE AN INDICATION OF QUALITY WHEN BUYING WINE?

The factors that affect the price of wine are many, and wine prices in each country vary enormously, but include:

- ❦ land prices
- ❦ winery equipment
- ❦ labour costs
- ❦ packaging
- ❦ bottling
- ❦ marketing
- ❦ distribution
- ❦ taxes and duties
- ❦ fashion
- ❦ perception
- ❦ popularity

The answer in short is, no, not really. You are more likely to pay a premium for a wine from a known region — and a winemaker is more likely to charge one — in the same way you might not pay as much for an unknown designer, even though the quality is just as good. Land costs in the iconic regions — Napa, Burgundy, Bordeaux and Champagne — are astronomical, while labour costs in some countries are less than others. It's more like a dynamic formula than an exact one; there are many variables and factors, unique to every market, that have an impact on the final price.

## RELEASE DATES

An old wine is not always a better version of its younger self. Some wines are made to age, while others aren't. But those that are set aside for ageing must be capable of it, built for it and stored well during the ageing process; a perfectly good wine can be ruined under bad storage conditions.

I've often thought that wines that are designed to age well are a bit like the second-most-popular group in high school – which is about exactly where you want your kids to be when they finish their secondary school tutelage. Kids who peak in high school get credit that's a little out of proportion for what they've achieved. Oh, it's not their fault, pretty little things – but they do get a lot of kudos for some fairly light and breezy achievements. Kids who are behind that level of popularity when they graduate have to work harder – to their benefit. They learn to endure completely unfair setbacks, to work on a more interesting and measured personality and to develop a sense of delayed gratification. Like spectacular wines crafted for endurance, they might get less attention upon release, but they age beautifully.

❦  TASTING NOTES  ❦

❦  A wine built to age is often less approachable upon release than those
made for immediate consumption; it might lack generosity of fruit, be
too high in acid or oak, which both soften over time, or it might just be a
simpler version of the complex version of its future self.

❦   Wines that are built to age must be stored well. Even the most
magnificent versions of both wines and people can be ruined with poor care.

# RESTRAINED WINES

A term that many use to describe wines that exhibit a sort of
subtlety of expression is 'restrained'. Conducting yourself
with grace while maintaining a considered position is a quality
that I think takes time to appreciate in life. It's one of life's anomalies that it takes all we have not to put everything in, to avoid
showy displays of emotion so as not to cheapen the beauty of it.

When I taste restrained yet beautiful wines, they always remind
me of that quiet specialness between two things that is captured
by John Donne in his poem that counsels his love for a temporary
separation:

'So let us melt, and make no noise,
No tear-floods, nor sigh-tempests move;
'Twere profanation of our joys
To tell the laity our love.'

## SANGIOVESE

W e'd barely been shown to our table when she asked, 'Are
you drinking tonight?'

It was just the two of us for dinner. I organised a restaurant
I thought she would love – quality food, closer to classic than
fusion, and an environment that was robust enough to allow us to
use our hands to talk.

'Absolutely, it's almost Christmas!' The buzz from the restaurant started to charge me. I was feeling relaxed and ready to
devour the night. 'So, how are things?'

'Really good.' As we spoke the waiter brought the wine list and
menu.

'You choose,' she said, and handed the wine list to me. Pre-
Christmas dinner, an inadvertent sense of celebration, big-hearted
Italian food – I'd imagined the flavours all day. Savoury, garlicky,
oily mouthfuls; generous serves spilling from plates; shared
starters and broken bread. 'I'll have a bottle of the Chianti.'

'Not for me. Maybe just get a glass.'

'Sorry?'

'No, I might sit.'

'Come on, we'll get something else. You must have a drink.
What about a white – a pinot grigio? Something sparkling –
a prosecco?'

Frowning, a theatrical but faux-thinking face. 'No, I'll definitely sit.'

She gave the wine list back, and the waiter left with his order of one lonely glass.

Finally settled, she was ready to open the evening: 'So, where were we last time, you must tell me *everything*.' I was rolling by the time my drink came, which was red, earthy, savoury and complex enough to match the situation.

We spoke of our searches for a meaningful life, the search for a calling, something worthy.

We both had a sip of my wine. She waved away my offer of getting her a glass of her own and nodded for me to go on.

This again. It's not just wine – it happens with food as well. I'm asked to order and told not to be shy. But when it comes, the abundance is not matched. 'You go ahead,' she encourages, 'tell me what's good.'

I ignore it and serve a bit of everything – rocket salad, crunchy bruschetta, and a small mound of spaghetti bolognese – texture, flavour, crunch and aroma. She serves her own and her portions looked mean and lonely on the plate.

I eat and I chat, and with another sip I ponder my wine. I'm grateful for

## THE BLOOD OF JOVE

Sangiovese is Italy's most popular red variety, and the main variety in Tuscany's Chianti classico and Brunello di Montalcino wines – though it's also grown in other countries, including America and Australia. Sangiovese (its name derived from Latin for 'the blood of Jove') brims with cherries, herbal savouriness, tobacco, spice and a mouthful of famous delightfully drying tannins. Given this, you can imagine how wonderfully it goes with pizza, grilled meats and hearty tomato-based pastas. No? Well, try it – it really does.

the wine's ability to take me away. What other drink can provide such company?

The food was quietly spectacular, and the pleasure it gave me felt intentional and kind. I thought beyond my companion to the chef and the winemaker, the vineyard, the soil ... ah, Tuscany: wild earth, bright berries, a grip that won't let go. Is this what you smell like? How you feel? One day I'll come to find out. For them and their work, I ate and I drank.

'And the writing? You must tell me all about it.'

We kicked conversations around for a while but I was long gone, having let my wine take me elsewhere.

Gradually, the leftover spaghetti stiffened and the oil on the plate stopped shining. When the waiter came to clear and straighten the table, he offered the desert menu and asked: 'How is everything, ladies?'

'Perfect,' I said, still among the rolling hills, olive groves and pencil pines of Tuscany.

## SAUVIGNON BLANC

S auvignon blanc is like the white wine 'It' girl: a perfect French pedigree, a place in the AOC, and an impeccable reputation sullied through a recent spate of overexposure. But it wasn't always this way. Sauvignon blanc's spiritual home is the Sancerre region of the Loire Valley in France. The grape has lived there for centuries, being nurtured into a gentle, refreshing, sometimes steely wine made to pair wonderfully with all manner of food that sits at the light end of the spectrum.

In recent decades sauvignon blanc has been planted in New Zealand to startling results. New Zealand sauvignon blanc, especially when grown in the Marlborough region, produces a style that's pronounced, pungent and crisp – and it took wine-loving ladies by storm. On the good side, sauvignon blanc is wonderfully fresh, clean, crisp summer drinking – on the too-much side, it's like walking out of the movies into bright bright daylight.

## 🍇 TASTING NOTES 🍇

🍇 All those who guzzled sauvignon blanc by the bottle, with scant attention for anything but a bright and fresh white wine, were doing exactly what people are suppose to do with sauvignon blanc – enjoying it.

🍇 Sauvignon blanc works well as an aperitif or matched with seafood, sunny days, casual catch-ups and a good coastal view.

🍇 For a sauvignon blanc with a difference, fume blanc is made in a quieter style and some even use a portion of old oak to give versions texture and complexity.

---

## SAVOUR THE SEASONS

Nature has a very particular set of objectives that all living things need to fulfill, each season, for a healthy and happy existence.

But these days technology, accounting cycles and a full diary have let us wander from what nature intended. We override the seasons by sourcing whatever we want from the Global Supermarket. We don't feel the seasons, just the temperatures. Inconsistencies in the weather become inconveniences to our routine, and most of us work to calendar deadlines, not seasonal ones. We have become less connected but more productive ... or so we think.

As natural beings, we *are* part of nature – and just as affected by the seasons as the birds, vines or the flowers. It doesn't take much introspection to acknowledge just how different you feel from one season to the next – how yearnings and longings and instincts change.

I mentioned this to someone recently, how our dispositions and instincts change according to the season and they said, 'Yes, but it's the weather that makes you feel like that.' Yes, precisely.

Consider a vine – each season, and *because* of the season, it has things it must do to survive and thrive. Just as a vine has jobs to complete each season that are fundamental to a healthy life, so do we. Eastern philosophy is rooted in this idea – the harmonising with nature for a happy life.

When you think about that, it makes wonderful sense, especially when you reflect on the cycle of the vines and what we can learn from it ...

*It's spring fever. That is what the name of it is. And when you've got it, you want — oh, you don't quite know what it is you do want, but it just fairly makes your heart ache, you want it so!'*

—*Mark Twain*, Tom Sawyer, Detective

## Spring

The phase of spring starts in space, when one side of the Earth moves closer to the sun. As it turns, it's like pulling up the blind and letting daylight in on a room full of sleeping children. As this happens, the temperature rises, heating the Earth's surface and the soil temperature. This wakes the vine from dormancy, and the sap in the plant starts running. Look closely at a vine in spring and you can see little buds on the end of the vines start to swell with water – ready, literally, to burst. Zoom in even closer and you'll see drops of water oozing from the pruning cuts: the vine's 'blood' flowing again. But the most significant act for a vine in spring is budburst – when small shoots burst from the buds, marking the end of dormancy and the beginning of a new cycle of life.

For people, as it is for vines, spring is a time of regeneration. It's the time for us to get busy, to execute the plans prepared for in autumn and put to rest while we slumbered through winter.

It's a time for conversations to flow and socialising to begin, for outdoor activity and a building of energy, for feasting our eyes on all of nature's joy and embracing a new cycle of life.

### Things to do in spring

Spring is where the cycle starts again. There is a lot of work to be done to help the vines in this new cycle of life: ploughing and spraying the vineyards, positioning new shoots for growth, and trimming to avoid excess foliage and protect the new buds against spring frosts.

It's a time to start executing the plans of growth.

## THINGS TO DO IN SUMMER

Summer is the quietest time in the vineyard – the main aim is to let the vines flower, fruit and then ripen. It is the winegrower's hope to leave the fruit on the vine for as long as possible to achieve that perfect balance between acid and sugar, while avoiding any natural threats such as disease, problems from excess rain, too much heat, or damage from hail, pests or wild animals. A lot of the work during summer is in preparing the winery for harvest – cleaning and testing equipment, loading up the stereo with new music, recruiting cellar hands and getting things in order for that busy time of harvest.

## SUMMER

Summer is the time of luxurious growth and ripening, of turning hard green grapes and their austere acids into sweet, juicy and plump bunches. The sun's warm and generous rays rest gently on the vine leaves, which are as wide as plates and as strong as vinyl, acting as both solar panels and shade for the plumping grapes. Vine rows look like rows of lush green jungle. Underneath the leaves, the grapes use the energy taken in from the leaves and stored from autumn the previous year to turn from a bright lime-green to a mottled mix, and eventually to their mature colour.

Summer for people is also a time of luxurious growth: late nights and early mornings, lots of social activity, adventure, travel, creativity, expansion; devouring ripe fruit and absorbing the sun's warmth just like grapes ripening in the sun. It's all about bringing to fruition all those wonderful plans you started in spring.

*'Summer afternoon ... summer afternoon ... the two most beautiful words in the English language.'*

—Henry James

## AUTUMN

I n the vineyard, autumn is a time of harvest, or 'vintage', collecting the fruits of the year's work. A frenzy of workers fights off threats and manages nature's moods – rot, rain, frost or hail – to ripen the fruit to perfection before relieving the vines of their fruit. This can span days, weeks or months, depending on size of vineyard, varieties planted, weather conditions and local climate. Once the vines are parted from their fruit, and while the winemakers continue the remarkable process of transforming grapes into wine, the vines prepare to shut up shop, collecting the last of the sun's energy, tucking it away for spring.

Just like after harvest, autumn for us is a time for slowing down, reflecting, taking stock and preparing for the long dark of winter, when everything natural sleeps. In Chinese philosophy, autumn is considered the natural end of the cycle and a time of courage and sadness: courage to continue on with plans, despite the melancholy, and sadness for the natural end of another cycle,

### THINGS TO DO IN AUTUMN

Autumn is crucial to complete the ripening of the fruit. Of course, vintage is the main event in this season. The critical thing is to pick grapes that are physiologically ripe, with sugar and acid in perfect balance. That's assuming things are going well. You also need to account for rot, rainfall, hail damage, under-ripe fruit and frost.

When the grapes come into the winery, the winemaking process begins. Crushing, fermenting, bubbling and transforming grapes into wine. This usually starts in September–October in the Northern Hemisphere, and February–March in the Southern Hemisphere.

Once the fruit is picked, the vines make a last rush for energy and the leaves store as much sunlight as they can for next spring. The roots make a quick rush outwards just to get as ready as they can for next time.

the dying of foliage, the shortening of the days and the dimming of the light. As Ezra Pound described it, it's 'a sweet sadness'. It's where nature intended us to pause, William Cullen Bryant's 'year's last, loveliest smile.'

## WINTER

### THINGS TO DO IN WINTER

Landscapes become bare and bleak as trees drop their foliage and shed their harvest. In the vineyard, after leaf-fall (when the vines shed their leaves — which have now done their work — to conserve their energy for the winter), vines are pruned, old canes removed and newer ones trained and prepared for spring.

As the bracing cold comes, the leaves drop, the sap in the vines descends into the roots and the vine goes to sleep. While the vines slumber, workers prune organise them for when they shoot again in spring. The vines will stay here in dormancy for several months, until the Earth makes that crucial turn again, and one side of it moves closer to the sun and the cycle starts again.

Winter gets a hard time from many, but I often wonder if people might enjoy winter more if they did what we were supposed to do: bunker down, eat hearty foods, drink thick red wine and hibernate, at least some of the time. I know it's difficult these days to hole up — no matter how much your instinct craves it — but winter really is a time for introspection, resting, storing energy for the long months ahead. Remember, like vines, it's a time to rest and conserve your energy for the  busy and productive parts of the year.

## Winter freeze

Vines are hardy plants, surviving in a range of conditions, including fairly marginal climates. Within these climates a vine is able to endure challenging seasonal weather including hail, searing heat and even ice. It has many ways to protect itself against such extremes. For example when the vine gets really hot, it shuts down to avoid any stress, like someone exposed to too much trauma. But one thing that will kill vines is extreme cold. When the temperature drops to minus 20 degrees Celsius, the sap in the veins of the vine freezes and, like frozen water in a pipe, it swells up and breaks the veins – killing the vine. Whenever I hear that I always think, what an awful way to go.

### Protecting vines

Vines can be protected against the damage caused by extreme cold by careful site selection, as well as the rare practice of burying them in the soil during autumn. This is because the soil temperature stays warmer than the air temperature.

*'I wonder if the snow loves the trees and fields, that it kisses them so gently? And then it covers them up snug, you know, with a white quilt; and perhaps it says "Go to sleep, darlings, till the summer comes again."'*

—*Lewis Carroll,* Through the Looking-Glass, and What Alice Found There

## SCORES

Scoring wine, like scoring most things in life, is a loaded and complicated issue. In recent decades, the wine score has become one of the most significant forms of judgement and influence on a wine – some say controversially so.

Wine-scoring systems come in a number of forms: five stars (or wine glasses or bottles, or other quirky wine-related symbols); out of twenty; and the most popular and influential wine system, the 100-point scale popularised in the 70s by wine writer Robert Parker. It was taken up in America with gusto, and is slowly making its way to other parts of the world.

On one hand, using a concise and digestible indicator of quality has merit. It has helped many cut through clutter and noise to understand something in a language they speak: a score of 95 out of 100 is universally understood.

What's more, many might not otherwise buy wines – especially wines of such quality – if their score were not so easy to understand. After all, isn't one of the barriers to wine engagement the series of communication hoops people have to jump through in order to understand wine? Wine scores, in many ways, fast-track this process. Not only do they speed up purchasing, but they also allow you to get to the very best wines faster than if you read and researched your way there. We are able to do so without judgement with fine-quality shoes, restaurants and cars – why not with wine?

Because this is wine and life, and neither of these things – least of all the two combined – is simple.

I definitely see the usefulness of scores, and their ability to sell wine, but I think it should be only one part of the story.

Just as I have trouble choosing favourites, I have trouble pinpointing anything down to such a precise degree. What's more, I know *I* have never done well being scored on numbers, so I feel the least I can do is try to understand the complete picture for others – even if those 'others' are bottles of wine.

I also can't help but wonder if wines should get extra points for their backstory. Some wines are more astonishing because of what they have come from – wines made from war-torn landscapes and cultures; wines made as experiments, in secret, with particular philosophies; or through plain hardship, like a person from a tough background. If their 85 points were harder to get, don't they deserve more? Are the thoroughbreds with perfect breeding and immaculate grooming better horses? Perhaps they run faster and look sleeker, but we liked Seabiscuit better.

For me, wine is way too complex for a number to be enough. It's not because I'm seeking some sort of wine egalitarianism, no matter what the quality – not at all. I'm all for finding absolute heroes; I just don't know that I've ever seen one that's perfect.

*'A creature may never be a perfect being,
but may be a perfect creature.'*

*—C.S. Lewis*

# ❧   TASTING NOTES   ❧

## THE DEBATE SURROUNDING SCORES
### FALLS A LITTLE LIKE THIS:

❧   *How can you reduce anything to a number?* This seems to be a
dilemma of modern life, but when it comes to wine, it's even
more complex. Given how subjective an act tasting is, and how
it draws on so many other ethereal layers and complexities, is
it really possible to reduce it to a meaningful number? To me
it's like trying to reduce great art or literature or nature to a
number. Not only is it hard, it kind of misses the point.

❧   *You miss the context.* A wine without context is like a person
without a backstory. Scored wines are typically tasted in sterile
environments, often blind and with nothing of the wine's
background known. Many argue this is precisely the benefit of
scoring — it is a judgement based solely on the wine's merits. But
many wines need a certain context to shine — be it their local
cuisine, or environment, or history — and may not score highly
in a judging environment.

❧   *Some wines are made to score well in a judging environment.* Some argue
the importance of wine scores in recent decades has influenced
the way wines are being made, so that they perform better in
scoring conditions. When wines score highly, they sell more
and for a higher price. Some winemakers, it has been suggested,
make wines with higher alcohol, deeper colour and greater
intensity — traits that get you noticed in the line-up. Is this
wrong, or merely competitive? These discussions run deep into
questions of authenticity, culture and the globalisation of wine.

❧   *You might miss a very good thing.* In the rush for buying the best
wines, many people ignore wines that are less than 90 points,
many of which might still be classified as 'very good wines with

finesse and polish' or something similar; that is, *very good* wines are sometimes left behind. If you go through life with that view, you'll end up missing some *very good* stuff — and sometimes, 'very good' is a lot better than most. I can't be sure if I have ever tasted a 100-point wine, yet I have been moved by thousand-point moments with wines that probably scored much less than 90.

## SHIFTING LANDSCAPES

For some reason that only she knows, Mother Nature has a certain order of where things should and shouldn't go.

I imagine she wrote some sort of master plan with everything mapped out: areas where cold things belong, where deserts thrive, perfect matches and regions for animals, plants, oceans, deserts and humans, like the perfect seating plan for the entire world.

But as we know, things don't always run according to plan. There has been a lot of re-shuffling from what was outlined on the original blueprint. For example, despite the plan, humans insist on penetrating many regions they're not meant to be, and not always successfully.

Vines too have areas where they can exist and, within that, places where certain vines don't just exist, but thrive. These places vary wildly between varieties – somewhere that is a good place to grow pinot noir is not necessarily conducive to growing tempranillo. Just as people are testing the limits of where they can go on Earth, so too are winemakers testing where vines thrive.

This reshuffling is being played out in many places, but perhaps nowhere more so than in Australia. A decade-long drought, changing environmental conditions, a series of extreme weather patterns, an over-reliance on French varieties, and the threat of climate change and all that goes with it – including less water, rising temperatures, earlier picking dates and a potential change in wine styles – have caused many to wonder about their next course of action.

As a result, many winemakers are now experimenting with varieties more suited to certain regions, with exciting results. These newer varieties are those that thrive in similar climates and conditions in other parts of the world, and are an attempt to realign with Mother Nature's blueprint.

For example, some southern Italian varieties, including fiano, vermentino and nero d'Avola, are perfectly happy growing in dry, arid conditions, so are being grown in warmer, drought-affected areas of northern Victoria where they are better suited to, and put less strain on, the environment than some other varieties. The first plantings of assyrtiko, originally from Santorini in Greece, have occurred in South Australia's Clare Valley, while the Spanish variety tempranillo is well established in and suited to McLaren Vale. As the varieties become available to winegrowers, the evolution will continue.

## ❦  TASTING NOTES  ❦

THOSE THAT BELIEVE IN CLIMATE CHANGE PREDICT THAT THE
INCREASE IN TEMPERATURE AS A RESULT OF GLOBAL WARMING
WILL AFFECT A RANGE OF FACTORS IN WINEMAKING:

❦  The increased heat will ripen grapes earlier, which means
earlier picking times, affecting which varieties can be grown in
certain areas and what wine styles these varieties are made in.
For example, a shiraz grown in a warm climate will produce a
wine with very different qualities to one that is grown in a cool
climate.

❦  Water shortages and extreme weather will become more
probable, as a result of the temperature increases. This is not
just an Australian issue – wine regions the world over may also be
affected, especially those places that are already on the margins
of Mother Nature's blueprint.

❦  While some places may become too warm or dry, others that
are currently too cold may, for the first time, be warm enough to
grow grapes.

---

# SHIRAZ

O utside the bistro was the coldest winter the city had experienced in a decade.

The two girls sat at the bar and chatted while they scanned the
menu for dinner. They spoke of busy work schedules and how
much they looked forward to dinner.

## Shiraz or syrah?

One of the world's most lauded red wine varieties, shiraz grows well, and distinctively, in most wine-growing places. Shiraz is also known as 'syrah', as it's referred to in its spiritual home, the Rhône Valley in France, and some other parts of the world.

Whatever it's referred to is usually determined by how it's grown and what style it's made in. For example, in Australia, the Barossa Valley and McLaren Vale are world renowned for producing big, powerful shirazes with flavours rich with dark berries, chocolate and spice. In the cooler Yarra Valley, many growers call it 'syrah' to signal the different style of the same variety: still lush with dark berries, pepper and spice, but often lighter bodied, more perfumed and elegant.

They ordered sensible food for such a night – hearty and nourishing osso bucco and a bottle of shiraz. The wine was poured and sat, dark and serious and brooding, in the large round glass.

The smaller one took a sip and said it was 'delicious' to no-one in particular before she slid off her scarf, rubbed her neck, flopped back on her chair and took another mouthful.

Their conversation was light for a while – work, the weather, a new dress – then the taller one leaned forward and touched her friend's forearm. 'Honey, you don't have to tell me this if you don't want to,' she said, her head falling to one side.

'No it's fine,' the smaller one said, taking another sip of her wine, seeming to draw strength from the intensity of the shiraz. At first she spoke in a low voice, but as the noise of the restaurant and the drama in the story rose, her voice did too. All the while her friend nodded and sipped, looking on sympathetically.

There was a long and shocking story that life had somehow embroiled her in. I didn't hear many details but I recognised the pain as universal.

The waiter filled their glasses of wine as they drank and talked, sometimes breaking the noisy hum of the restaurant with comments like, 'Do you know what that means? What the implications are for my family?' The whites of the girl's eyes revealed shock and fear, while the taller one occasionally rubbed her friend's back as comfort. In the middle of the ordeal had been an engagement party in a vineyard where she'd had to put on a brave face despite her grief, smiling and making a toast while she held back tears.

She spoke of the strain of keeping this painful thing down and away from anyone else, and how it was taking its toll on her, her family, her work.

I looked around the restaurant at other tables, other pairs, couples and clusters drinking wine, some laughing, some talking intently, everyone now in the core of their conversations.

It never ceases to amaze me, I thought, whether by survival, ingenuity or necessity, how different people's personal lives can be from the external stories they show to the world. As I looked around and watched people talk, I wondered about all that real life being spoken about – behind the wine – at every table.

*'In three words I can sum up everything*
*I've learned about life. It goes on.'*

—Robert Frost

## SHOUTS

It was the summer holiday toward the end of high school. A girl-friend and I moved into her parents' holiday house for a bit of the summer – it might have been a month – to have a working holiday. As is often the case over long summers with little to do and even less life experience, it was rich with small lessons about life and living.

My friend was the third child of four children, and the only girl. This meant that for our entire friendship we were surrounded by lots of boys – her brothers and friends of her brothers – who at the time seemed more like men than the boys in ties who went to school near us. And they knew it. While our male school friends hung about in blazers and sports uniforms, these boys were into rumbles, boys' nights, trucks, toolboxes, trades and Friday night shouts. They had names like Broady, Corker, Rossco, Soda and Ando – they were *The Outsiders* in Australian cars.

Perhaps due to the initiations they had endured as apprentices, or just because they were boys, they took delight in tormenting the schoolboys we tried to take out. 'We're doing you a favour,' they would say. 'Just checking him out for you.' A particular point of delight was inviting these lads to have a drink, which meant befriending them, offering them a drink, and then slowly, steadily out-drinking them until the poor things got ridiculous. Many passed out; few passed muster.

I always thought these older boys were so kind to look out for us, but I now understand what it is for a boy to have a 'little sister and her friends' around.

As things got closer to Christmas and New Year's Eve, people poured into town like a tidal wave rolling onto land, filling every spare space and creating new ones. Queues crumbled out of restaurants and into the streets, carparks became jammed and roads became carparks. Makeshift signs for 'no parking', 'free parking' and 'campsites full' leaned against gum trees and fence posts.

On weekends, the boys would come down from town and stay at the house. During those weekends we sat on the back deck of the house, high on the hill, and told stories that, for that summer at least, became lore and legend.

One of the boys, a friend to this day, shared other supposed insights: how to tell if someone is a good guy, and the importance of the shout – a 'round' in other parts of the world. One's behaviour in a shout, I was told, was an insight into someone's character in life. Or, as I thought many years later, 'Give me the man in a shout, and I'll give you the man in life.'

On that back deck we also heard of tales from the pub where the much-older brothers would disappear for entire afternoons and long into the night, appearing at breakfast the next day with sore heads, a few whispers and lots of laughs.

The pub was a central part of the boys' visit to the coast, but still out of bounds for my girlfriend and me. It remained a mysterious place at the end of the main street. I remember one night, after finishing our shift, my friend and I wandered to the foreshore and hung on the swings in the playground. The wind carried the music from the pub, the lights twinkled in the distance, the waves crashed on the beach. Swinging and dancing and laughing at how uncool it was that we were in the children's playground while friends were at the pub, I guess it was just that time of life – we were too old for one place, but not old enough for another.

One particular weekend, I was alone and the boys invited me to the pub. As the New Year's Eve crowds grew, getting into the pub while under-age felt like escaping from Alcatraz. But on this night the boys insisted.

The main entrance, opposite the surf club and the beach, was at the top of about ten stairs upon which the bouncers stood, shoulder to shoulder. For me, underage, guilty, and looking both in equal measure, it was like walking to the gallows.

'Not the front, go around the back,' the boys said. I was told someone would meet me around the corner and down the lane near the rubbish bins.

'Seriously? I'll just go home,' I said, happily conceding to a walk along the beach. I wasn't in that much of a rush to go to the pub.

'Go 'round, *now*!'

Inside, in the magnificent beer garden overlooking the ocean and the winding coastline, the boys had executed a master plan. Having befriended the bouncers during the low season, they convinced them that the beanbag-sized boulders that dotted the garden, like meteors flung from space, were a hazard. As mates, they offered to help.

For the next fifteen minutes, a small army of bouncers and friends, like sportsmen in the Colosseum, picked up gigantic boulders and moved them from one spot to another, while I was lifted over the back fence accessed by a laneway.

Inside, I was swept into a whole new and exciting universe. The pub, at least their part of it, was like a small village with its own rhythms and order. At the centre of this universe was a large wooden table surrounded by bench seats brimming with people, some only half fitting on. I was squeezed in between two of the boys and told to stay seated, for fear of being caught. Like outer rings of our universe, people lingered, passing drinks and lighters, talking loud and laughing hard over the music, the energy drawing new people in like the pull of the moon on the ocean.

In even rhythms, precipitated by gentle actions as slight as a tilt of the hand or raise of the eyebrow, people went to the bar for their round, returning with stacks of glasses and swaying jugs of beer, round after round, back and forth.

Across the road from the beer garden, the ocean continued a rhythm that ensured order remained, wave after wave, crashing the white frothing waves on the beach; and inside, as each glass and frothing jug landed on the table, the rhythm of the shout did exactly the same thing.

### ❧    Tasting notes    ❧

A shout, as it is known in Australia and New Zealand, is the social custom of buying a round of alcoholic beverages.

My friend from this story wrote me a two-thousand-word email about the rules and etiquette of the shout.
Here are those that I think might be useful:

❧    Make sure all participants agree they are in the shout.

❧    For smooth shouting, all participants should try to drink the same thing, or at least the same size.

❧    You can't skip out before your round. 'This is the number one no-no'. 'But what if they leave for an emergency?' I asked. 'They have to buy a full round for everyone, then leave.' 'Seems a little harsh.' 'Rules are rules.'

# SLURPING

I t's a wonder I attend wine tastings at all, given how much I loathe eating noises.

This sensitivity probably came about because my uncle – who smoked a pipe even until it was hard to justify without a tweed deerstalker and a monocle – used to breathe quite heavily out of his nose. When he ate, it was like the sound of an air mattress deflating.

Dinner times were torture. I often felt a whole side of me go numb, as I tried to shut off all sensory activities by giving myself a temporary paralysis on one side of my body. Which probably just made me appear obtuse and disengaged.

The evolution of my phobia into adulthood has been the hardest; now I can hear the sound of a person eating with as much sensitivity as a hunting dog can a high-pitched whistle.

It still lingers.

Forks scraping on plates are like fingernails down a chalkboard, a bag of chips while I'm reading a book on a quiet Saturday afternoon feels like a personal attack, a slurp of soup ... well, let's just say a bowl of pho can be a struggle.

Movies are the worst; all those people with all those wrappers. What are they doing with them?

PUT THEM DOWN AND SORT THEM OUT LATER! I want to yell.

They do eventually put them down, right after they've scraped every miserly crumb and lick of MSG residue from the wrapper, ending it off with a best-of-three competition to see who can make the most elaborate wrapper-swan using the ancient craft of origami.

So it's any wonder I don't run screaming from the first sound of someone slurping, sorry, *aerating*, their wine at a formal tasting. Maybe it's the years of weathering it that makes it ok.

What is that noise, anyway? A cross between a bath being let out, a sprinkler, and the sound you made to your friends in school if you suspected them of sucking up to the teacher.

**A CIRCUS IN YOUR MOUTH**

Aerating the wine in your mouth enhances the wine's flavour and natural aromas. It's the same reason wine is swirled in the glass before tasting. When aerating the wine in your mouth, the noise is, apparently, optional.

And it's quite astonishing that the one industry that gets, and perhaps deserves, the biggest rap for being a little, well, proper, makes that sound en masse.

There is a point to it, you know. It's to break up the surface of the wine to release the flavour molecules so that you get a bit of an extra hit of flavour and aroma. And when you are assessing or appreciating wine, it's good to squeeze as much as you can out of those first assessing sips.

You know, despite my general aversion to eating noises, I have embraced the slurp; quite enjoy it, actually. In the same way that you realise, when you're gardening, that it's much more fun to get dirty and wet all over the place than to try to fuss about keeping neat.

Being at a wine tasting and really rolling that sip of wine around your mouth is a small yet liberating gesture. It's no wonder I forgot the noise and embraced it.

## SMELL THE ROSÉS

'Ta-daa!' she said, swinging open the door and twirling her arm behind her. 'You like?'

'Well, get out of the way so I can come in and have a look.'

I wandered in and plonked down two bottles of wine. One was a chardonnay to match the casual dinner of pork we were having. I was about to open the other when she dragged me off for the 'official tour' of the two-bedroom flat.

As she showed me around I noticed that she had already settled in. Her efficiency is beyond impressive – always has been. I have relied on her lightning-quick box ticking to get my own tasks done: researching a trip, checking out flights. She looks at To Do lists like a sprinter sizing up a racetrack.

'It's so good you have your own place now,' I said as we looked in doors and peeked in cupboards.

'You're telling me.'

Just a year ago she was suffering terribly. She had asked me, in an unusually formal email, to meet her for regular laps of The Tan walking track to help her through her depression. Walking was one of the few things she could face. When I met her on those hazy afternoons, she was so numb and absent that I often felt more like a chaperone than a companion. Mostly she hid beneath her cap, looking down as I watched the path ahead for both of us.

Not knowing what to do, I took her to a place where I have sought my own solace. Instead of walking The Tan with the frenzy of lycra-wrapped runners, football teams in training and girls walking as a catch-up, we went into the quiet and magnificent Royal Botanic Gardens. There we wove through the lawns to the rose garden: a small patch of grass with several rectangular boxes of roses walled by evergreen trees. Every week until daylight saving ended, I walked my friend there to literally stop and smell the roses.

On still nights the perfume hung around the petals like an aromatic fog. Only some of the roses were strong enough to hold the perfume within the frills of their petals. We always shared the roses we smelt, cupping them and saying, 'Smell this one,' 'Try this one,' 'This one is beautiful.'

Eventually it became more winter than autumn, and then it was just plain winter. The petals dropped and daylight saving stopped.

So to see my friend a year on, in her own flat, happy, having wrestled the demons that ruled her for a while, really was something.

'Ok, that's all there is to show,' she said. Box ticked. 'So, come on. What did you bring to drink?'

I poured us a glass of the second wine I had brought, a rosé. I held up the lovely pink glass to her. 'Stop and smell the rosés?'

## The Delights of Rosé

There are many ways to describe the flavours and textures of rosé — watermelon, strawberry, ripe red-berry fruits. Others say that it's such a perfectly casual wine that you'd only ruin it by adding technical descriptions to it and dragging it toward areas of wine connoisseurship it doesn't need to be near. But in the interests of encouraging you to try it, because I think you should, I describe rosé like this: that moment on a warm summer afternoon — and it is summer and it is the afternoon — when you find a patch of grass or perhaps a comfortable chair outdoors where you can stretch your muscles, wiggle your toes, and feel the warmth of the sun on your skin as you lie back. As the sun moves onto your face and a calm moves through your body, you close your eyes and notice the soft pink glow that the sun makes as it lights up the delicate skin of your eyelids, and note how lovely this makes you feel. That's rosé.

❧ TASTING NOTE ❧

A PINK WINE MADE OF RED GRAPES, ROSÉ IS AS LOVELY TO
LOOK AT AS IT IS TO DRINK.

❧ Served chilled, rosé is also a delightful food match, pairing
deliciously with cold meats, fresh seafood, pasta
and any number of Asian dishes.

# SNOBS

U ntil recently, I didn't even think snobs were real – just caricatures played by James Spader in 80s movies starring Molly
Ringwald, written in when producers needed a morally bankrupt
character to steer the narrative toward the dark side for a while.
Which is probably why I don't fare well with them – because
everyone knows snobs come from Britain, not Hollywood.

Typically, snobs are attracted to wine like bees to honey, and
have been for years. Many would argue it's their fault it got so
complicated in the first place, but I don't think that's true. Wine is
a layered, beautiful, magical fusion of science, nature, philosophy,
pleasure and something unexplainable. Yes, it's complicated, but
all on its very own. Snobs are just aware of wine's social currency,
and so it remains as necessary an item in their portfolio of pretentious tricks as a school tie is to their box of most cherished posses-
sions, a whiff of misogyny to their attitude to women, and a club
membership to their list of life achievements.

When talking about wine with a snob, mentioning key phrases like 'score', 'critic', 'Europe' or 'a medal' is like the wine snob's manifesto. These criteria don't make them the best wines, but it can make them prestigious, which is really all snobs are after. Snobs are quite easy to buy for: just look for a noble variety, an award, an aged release and a hefty price tag.

*'A snob is someone who is blinded to the natural charms of meeting someone new because they are so busy making judgements ...'*

—The Debrett's Guide to Modern Manners

## SPITTING

No matter how long you have been in a sport or hobby, no matter how many qualifications you have or accolades adorn you, there is always one small gesture, unique to that interest, that shows how good you *really* are. Some skateboarders have that cool little flick they do to lift their board from the ground while they're still in motion as if they just said to their board, 'Up.' Some guitar players have a way, when they've finished playing, of sliding their

## YOUR SPITTING IMAGE

Spitting while tasting not only keeps you sober, but there is little benefit in swallowing wine, as there are no taste or flavour receptors in your throat.

The best way to get better at spitting is to practise – and the safest place do so is in the shower. Get a mouthful, take aim and spit forcefully, pursing your lips as you do so. You can make noise, but you're not supposed to dribble.

instrument around their body, like a dance partner in a tango, to rest it on their back, all early-days Springsteen-like. And some sailors, no matter what the conditions, can finger a rope into a bowline without even looking at it, let alone bothering with 'The rabbit hops out of the hole, goes around the tree, and back down the hole'. It's not the oceans they've crossed but the knot-tying that gives it away, just like it's not the albums the musician has sold, but the slide of the guitar that gives him his cool.

And, when it comes to wine, it's not the wines they've drunk or the competitions they've judged, but the long, precise, flying arc of their spit that lets you know the wine-taster who means business.

## STANDARD SERVES

A standard serve of wine is an elusive and complicated thing. As we know by now, nothing about wine is straightforward – wily little minx that she is – and trying to define a standard serve, or standard drink, or unit of alcohol, is like trying to define a standard serve of weather.

There are a several reasons for this.

First, alcohol content in wine varies significantly because the natural growing process determines how much sugar there is in the grapes. As this sugar is converted to alcohol during wine-making, it also determines how much alcohol there is in a wine. This measure is called 'Baumé' and typically eleven Baumé of sugar in a grape will convert to 11 per cent alcohol in the wine.

No matter how assiduous the viticulturalist is, it's challenging to control the percentage of alcohol by volume because it's hard to control how ripe the grapes get – you can manage what nature gives you, but not control it. As a result, alcohol in wine can vary from 8 per cent in some wines to 16 per cent in others.

Another complication is that the standard drink, typically set by a country's government, varies in each country. In Australia it's 10 grams of alcohol per serve, no matter if this comes in a shot glass or a litre of beer; in America it's 14 grams, while in England it's 8 grams.

Another twist is that to work out how much alcohol you have in a glass of wine requires a kind of riddle of numbers and maths that my brain doesn't deal well with. When I sit down to dinner, I can barely work out whether I want prosecco or champagne to start, let alone 'If a standard drink is 10 grams of alcohol, and this wine is 13 per cent alcohol by volume, how many standard drinks have I had over one and a half hours, with food, if I am on a train travelling at a thousand kilometres an hour?'

This is why I catch taxis everywhere. Some people say they're really expensive, that the costs really add up – given all the numbers involved with the calculations, I wouldn't know.

One thing you should know is that the faint lines across wine glasses in restaurants do not indicate a standard drink – they are for stock-keeping purposes, so sommeliers and managers can forecast and purchase the right amount of wine and know how many serves per bottle they will get. This does not indicate a standard unit of alcohol; in fact, one glass is most likely *at least* one standard serve of alcohol.

But the most complicating thing about the standard drink is the environment in which it is consumed. Recently, I have enjoyed wine with eight old friends at our first dinner together after two babies were born to people within the group; with another, to brainstorm new creative projects for the year ahead; to comfort another who is having a tough time at life; with a hundred others at a fortieth birthday party; and with a crew while sailing on a rough sea.

You see, that's the other tricky thing about working this out: in life there is no such thing as a standard occasion, so how on Earth can we match a standard serve?

## 🍇 Tasting notes 🍇

🍇 One glass of wine probably does not equal one standard drink – most likely, it's more.

🍇 What constitutes a legal standard drink varies between countries.

🍇 Wine can vary enormously in its alcohol content per bottle. As can your tolerance.

🍇 If in doubt as to how much alcohol you've had, you've probably had too much – so play it safe, catch a taxi; sign out of Facebook and, if you must, tell them you miss them in a private text.

# STATUS

I was in a taxi in Champagne, returning to my village after a winery visit. The driver was about fifty, had a short beard that might well have just been three-day growth, and seemed too big for the car, with his big hands, forearms as thick as thighs and large belly. Neither of us spoke the other's language so we engaged each other in the scenery – he pointed to something in a field, said one or two French words – I assumed the object or animal's name – and I would say 'Ahhhhh, merci' in that 'So *that's* what it is!' way. It was fun.

When we came to a village, the driver pointed out a large Provençal château. Set behind a thirty-foot white fence, it had two rows of five windows, white shutters open, with autumnal and trimmed ivy crawling neatly between them. I was later told it was the private château of one of the large champagne houses, used to accommodate VIP guests.

The driver again pointed at the house and said 'Huh' to get my attention. As I looked at him he started acting, turning his head from one shoulder to the other, dusting invisible dirt off his shoulders in two exaggerated flicks of his hand on each side. He pointed again to the house and then to me and said 'oui' in a lighter, friendly tone; then he pointed at himself in a more dramatic tone, almost a grunt, frowned and said 'non' and turned the corner of his mouth down to cement the insult, before driving us both on.

★          ✳          ✳          ★

✳          ★          ★

✳          ★          ★          ✳

That wine has a reputation for being a little status-driven is hard to argue with – it's for this reason that wine followers are some of the most parodied and mocked enthusiasts in the world.

But I'm not sure it's entirely fair. Not only because the idea of the wine snob is an outdated one that would be inaccurate to isolate to wine (if one is a wine snob, you can be sure it's not just with wine); but also because it's particularly inequitable to point the finger at wine, when these days the race for status is infused into just about every known topic, hobby, interest or idea that I can think of.

Of course a scramble for status is endemic in areas like business and money and suity things like that, but I have also noted a few surprising playing fields where the pursuit of status seems rife, and a little contrary to what it should be.

I hear people say parenting can be quite competitive: getting the babies to peacefully sleep through the night and recording off-the-chart percentile measurements, along with achieving or maintaining full exercise regimes for the mothers themselves, are all part of the race.

Yoga is another area where I was surprised to see an inference of status. If it's not the duration of the headstand, it's the number of classes taken this week alone, the amount of time spent in India or the organic-ness of the latest mass-produced yoga outfit. What happened to *namaste*?

And when did status leak into being smart, outside of academia? I don't mean *being* smart – hats off to anyone meeting their potential – I'm talking about claiming the image of intelligence with a pair of heavy glasses frames and using a wall of vintage paperbacks as a fashion accessory.

And then there's the glorification of busyness – surely that's a competition that no-one wins by winning?

You know, I want to say there's nothing wrong with this – it's just people being people, and maybe it's happened forever – but I think there's something wrong and a little bit upsetting about it all. Wrong because we are doing things for the wrong reasons; wrong because we are claiming virtues that are not yet ours; wrong because it is missing the point of having interests or pursuits at all.

I don't think this is new; I suspect that it's just more prevalent now because there are more things to buy and ways to signal which tribe you belong to. (Whether or not my taxi driver would believe me is another thing.)

But still: before pointing the finger at wine for its culture of examining and seeking out layers of quality, you might want to take a moment, think back to the last time you read a vintage existential-crisis paperback, and ask yourself: 'Why did I even read that?'

### 🍇 TASTING NOTES 🍇

🍇 That wine quality varies has been noted for centuries and, as a result, there have been many attempts to classify, list, state, define, order and cement the various levels of quality.

🍇 In the European Union, participating wine-producing countries designate wines as either Quality Wine or Table Wine. Each country within the EU has a system to determine criteria for each of these categories. There are twenty-one wine-producing countries in the EU, and all vary in their definitions and requirements of what makes a wine 'quality'.

🍇 Perhaps the most famous classification of wine quality is the Bordeaux Wine Official Classification of 1855 — known as the 1855 Classification — which was commissioned by Napoléon III for the Exposition Universelle de Paris to classify the wines of Bordeaux for visitors to the show. It still stands today, with only minor alterations to the original.

🍇 Outside Europe, which has the most formal system, are the show-judging system, wine scoring, and auction-house classifications. They are all attempts to define parameters of wine quality and, often inadvertently, create a hierarchy to wine quality.

## STORIES

P erhaps it was the relaxation that came from spending a day in the country, in a book-filled cottage that was set amongst paddocks of horses, that got my friends reflecting on wine: how they bought it and when they drank it. One declared herself a champagne girl. 'Only French. It tastes better and doesn't give me a hangover,' she said, a sudden spritz of energy running through her. The other proudly announced that she buys her wine according to the label because she finds it all a bit confusing.

'Besides,' she said, waving her hand like she was shooing a fly, 'it doesn't really matter.'

I was thinking how refreshing such definite and uncomplicated views on wine were when they said it: 'But I don't really know that much about wine so I've probably got no idea ...'

And there it was: the curtsey and concession to the gargantuan beast that is wine knowledge. It seems to happen a lot. It's both the appeal and the burden of wine that, in order to enjoy it, we believe we need to know something about it. Too often it feels as though we're not able to profess our love for the drink quite as breezily as we do for a bunch of flowers, a pair of boots or our new favourite song. We can't just love it, and tell others that this is so.

When it comes to wine, we feel compelled to know something about it in order to pass as a worthy wine-drinker. As if to prove how little we know, there is a corpus of literature, updated every single year, documenting just how much there is to know. No other gastronomical pursuit places so much weight on prerequisite information. Food certainly doesn't; in fact, most people are very comfortable talking about the seven-course degustation they had at a three-hat restaurant. But retelling a high-quality wine experience often elicits a more cautious response: 'I don't know much about wine ...' or 'I'm probably wrong ...' or, worse, 'Is this ok?'

The idea that having some knowledge means you will enjoy your wine more is one of the problems of wine. The other problem, of course, is that there is some truth to this. Because there *is* something miraculous about a wine that has lain sleeping for decades, performing again after a yawn and a stretch as it leaves the bottle for its next incarnation. There is admiration for a wine that comes from land planted to vine for two thousand years; nostalgia in knowing that only a certain grape, planted on a certain plot, will taste like that. It's captivating to think that the best sites for vineyards might yet be discovered. As I watched the horses meandering through the paddocks that afternoon, it occurred to me that the best sites might even be lying under the hooves of grazing animals.

When I pushed a little further, I learned that my friend loves good champagne because it reminds her of 'youth and liberty'. One of her favourite champagne stories is from when she was travelling through the French Alps with her family. It was part of a longer trip around the world that transformed them as individuals and as a whole. While there, she received news that her business had sold for a happy sum. She spent the night with friends, drinking bottle after bottle of vintage Dom Perignon, celebrating her extended liberty amongst the Alps before stumbling home, making enough noise to wake the glaciers from slumber.

My other friend, who buys wine based on the labels, divides them into two categories: 'a bit posh' and 'a little bit more posh'. It doesn't make much difference, because some of her best wines were drunk amongst a landscape as ancient and large as time itself. Some years earlier she had driven off in a 4WD with her family of four, for a twelve-month adventure around Australia. One year turned into three. They lived remotely, camping, home schooling and drinking the best wines of her life by an open fire in the middle of the outback, 'learning to be a family again'.

So sure, it is true that wine can be more enjoyable if you know something about it. But it's important to remember that the special hook that makes it more enjoyable can be your very own.

# TANNINS

T annins are responsible for that lovely grippy feeling on your gums and inner cheeks when you sip a glass of some red wines. In wine they come from the skins, seeds and stems of red grapes and, to a lesser extent, the oak that the wine is made or aged in. Some varieties, such as cabernet sauvignon, nebbiolo, tannat and shiraz, have a lot of tannins.

The amount of tannin in the wine is determined a bit by the grape and a lot by the winemaker. Like making a cup of tea, you can let the tea draw and extract out a lot of these tannins – which the winemakers do by leaving the skins and juice in contact with each other – or you can give it a quick dip, extracting only the gentlest whiff. Wines with lots of tannin are usually long-lived varieties, as tannins play an important role when it comes to ageing a wine.

## ☙ TASTING NOTES ☙

☙ As there is more skin contact in red wines, tannins have a much higher presence in red wines. They help to age a wine, and are what accounts for the sediment in an old wine.

⁕ When you taste a lot of young tannic wines, the sensation on your mouth and gums can be quite something. It reminds me of a dare my older brother and sister would throw me: to see how long I could hold a salt-and-vinegar chip on the inside of my bottom lip before the sensation became too much to bear. Which was never nearly as painful as when they tied me to the bunk and told me I was adopted.

## TASTING NOTES

'A shimmering pale straw colour, this wine has aromas of grapefruit, lemon, lime, citrus with mineral overtones and toasty oak notes. The palate is complex, continuing the citrus and weaving in notes of brioche and nuttiness, lingering long and lovingly on the palate and finishing with a generous acid backbone and length.'

The tasting note.

What a conundrum.

A blessing and a curse.

Is there anything that has at once caused so much trouble and joy for the wine industry and its followers?

Tasting notes have been mocked and imitated, laughed at and parodied. They are the most bewildering form of communication to the wine civilian and, probably after the price, the second most-read. If there is one feature of the wine industry's caricature that the civilian world knows about, it is the tasting note.

Funny thing is, this was what the wine industry came up with when they tried to take the fluff out of it.

I know.

So how did it come to this?

I suspect a few reasons, each of them in turn adding a new layer to the puzzle.

The first reason for this tricky reputation, I suspect, is what we know as connoisseurship. Although wine has been judged and assessed for centuries, it was largely for the purpose of quality. Given how rustic winemaking was back then, much of the wine would have been faulty or, at the very least, rough. Assessment back then was whether it was ok to drink, not to provide a flowery description of what it tasted like. Even when more complex assessments of quality were introduced, most famously with the 1855 Classification, the language for tasting notes as we know it today was still absent.

According to Steven Shapin in *The Tastes of Wine: Towards a Cultural History*, it was some time after the Classification that more elaborate language was used to evoke subjective feelings of how the wine tasted, peaking from the 1930s on with rather poetic wine language from writers such as André Simon and A.J. Liebling, although there were still no specific tasting notes.

It was not until some time between the 1950s and the 70s, when a wealth-driven lifestyle blossomed, that status and puffery were spun into the weave of wine assessment. The ornate language was increasingly used in an armoury of pretentious affectations. It was probably at this time that the wine snob was born.

However, during the 80s, and in an attempt to clear out the puffery and establish a less judgemental language, a group of scientists led by Professor Ann Noble at the University of California, Davis, created the aroma wheel. The aim was to take out the judgemental terminology in wine and identify those aromas that you can actually smell in wine, according to real flavour compounds that are present. Aromas were clustered together in groups and used as a kind of catalogue of acceptable references. It was here we were given the approved words with which to build our tasting notes – such as the one at the start of this entry, which could be written for chardonnay.

Since then, the industry of wine educators has rolled out a model of wine appreciation that includes both aspects. It teaches us that to enjoy and understand wine, we must know how to assess it; the aroma wheel gives us the permissible words with which to do so, and the wine education industry teaches us how to weave the two together in a clinical and non-judgemental manner, just like a wine judge.

All good additions, very well intentioned, and a clear explanation as to how we got here. But I am not sure the evolution of the tasting note is quite complete.

I can't help but think that, in our efforts to make the expression of wine more sensible, we have forgotten about the bits that make wine beautiful.

Wine has a powerful capacity to move us, to make us think deep thoughts and take us to places that no other drink does. To be forced to distil this to a scientific note underplays the joyousness of wine. For me, tasting in these technical ways makes loving wine a little bit harder, like kissing your love through iron bars – like marching when you want to dance.

Some wines require so much more from us. In fact, some wines are so extraordinary it would be insulting of us not to express more than an approved list of descriptors.

But how?

I once heard a non-wine literary writer speak of the challenge of writing about highly emotional situations. He described a moment for a character that was highly charged with love and joy and sentimentality. With no words to accurately articulate these feelings, he wrote an action to express it – the character ran and jumped into a river, hollering as he flew through the air and splashed into the water, sinking beneath its coolness. It was all he could do to express his joy.

Others say such moments of heightened emotion can only be expressed through poetry, a form that for centuries has expressed awe and beauty, sadness and love, and the magical spirit of things where rational sentences just wouldn't do.

I think wine is made up of so many of these moments of small and wondrous joys, and I am certain it is these moments of emotion and awe that make us love and cherish it.

The scientists did a good thing by evaporating the pretention and providing the language and giving the wine-show judges a method. It serves us well in moments of technical assessment, but is this really how we learn to enjoy wine?

If you are going to rely on a tasting note, do so – it's a helpful technique to begin to understand a wine. But don't forget the other bits, the bits beyond the technical, the bits that we turn up for.

Who knows? Maybe in the future, for the same wine described earlier, we'll see a note that combines the lot: 'Aromas of tropical stone fruits, including apricots and peaches, precede, woven with a lovely backbone of acid and minerality. The gentle French oak and alluring fruit flavours remember both the warmth and slow-ness of a golden sunset, while the acidity and minerality, the crisp, fresh edges of a bracing sunrise. It makes me want to pull the roll neck of my cable-knit sweater closer to my jaw, tilt my face toward the sun and softly shut my lids. "Like gold to ayery thinnesse beate" to the tunes of Debussy's *Claire de Lune*. Stay gold, chardonnay.'

' *"Speak English!" said the Eaglet. "I don't know the meaning of half those long words, and I don't believe you do either!"* '

—*Lewis Carroll*, Alice's Adventures in Wonderland

# ❧ Tasting notes ❧

A new way of analysing wine
(should you be that way inclined):

❧ Colour ...................................................................

❧ Aromas...................................................................

❧ Flavours.................................................................

❧ Acidity ..................................................................

❧ Tannins..................................................................

❧ Length ..................................................................

❧ Emotions................................................................

❧ Action...................................................................

❧ Poem/Book/Movie.........................................................

❧ Place....................................................................

❧ Music....................................................................

❧ Person...................................................................

# TECHNOLOGY

Technology is one of those things that we all object to until we learn to love it.

'Why do I need to tell everyone I'm eating my lunch?' 'I don't want people knowing where I am!' 'The newspaper online? But I've got one right here!'

Technology, in wine and life, might be our biggest frenemy yet. We're still working out if it's bad or good for us.

In life it has helped with so much – medicine, health, communication, travel, industry. But it has also challenged many special things we have given up too readily: free time, nature, solitude, alleged imperfections, happy meandering.

Much wine that is available in the world today would not be possible without technology: refrigeration and other processes that stop wine spoilage, which was a problem until a few decades ago, have helped improve wine quality the world over. Technology also helps in various areas of viticulture, including water management and irrigation, managing environmental threats and vineyard site selection.

But there are other techniques and technologies that have

made more cosmetic changes to wine and, just like in cosmetic surgery, there is much debate about just how authentic the end product is. Every layer of manipulation you add, some say, is a step away from authentic wine.

Perhaps one of the most debated trends in current winemaking is a turning away from so much controlling technology, and a return to winemaking with less or no human intervention.

I wonder if this is happening across prosperous societies in general; we all took up technology, but now we're not so sure about it. It reminds me of the debate around Western medicine versus alternative treatments. Some say Western medicine is bad for us; proponents argue that it is only because of it we now have the luxury of looking at more holistic ways of healing ourselves.

I guess, if it does go that way, that is one of the lovely things about wine; that you could still make it without any technology.

Actually, you can pretty much do anything without technology. The problem is, you just can't tweet about it.

## ❦  TASTING NOTES  ❦

❦  More an approach than a certified way of farming, the natural wine movement is about minimising human intervention in the winemaking process. This might include minimising or excluding additives, pesticides, and sulphates. As there is no 'natural' certification, this approach does draw some criticism for its flexible interpretation of the term 'natural'.

❦  These days technology allows winemakers to 'soften' wines with a technique called microoxygenation, add oak aromas using chips or staves rather than barrels, reduce alcohol content, eliminate pests in the vineyard, machine harvest and post photos every step of the way.

How much or how little you do in the winemaking process is up to individual discretion, which is why there is such a large range between 'natural', minimal intervention, commercial and modern styles of winemaking. Winemaking is like one of those mixing desks in a recording studio: there are a thousand things you can adjust to make a good album. Whether it's a good album or a mass-produced release is a whole other argument.

# TEMPRANILLO

## THE SPANISH BEAUTY

Tempranillo is Spain's star red variety, most famous in the wines of the Rioja and Ribera del Duero regions, though it's also made well in other parts of the world. A luscious mouthful of dark berries, herbs, earth, leather and spice, tempranillo can come with less of the tannin and acid that can make other reds seem more confronting. It's perfect for a plate of cold cuts on a night when the autumnal warmth is fading to a chill.

Knowing a little about some things in life is much more useful than knowing a lot about some others.

For example, I think it's far more impressive to be a graceless hack on the piano than it is to know everything about, say, human biology. Sure, it might save your life, but nothing says 'most popular guest' more than being able to slide in front of a piano late at night and knock out a set of classics.

The same can be said for cooking. Knowing how to reduce a sauce, make a jus or whip up a simple pasta with whatever is in the fridge is far more fetching than knowing the particulars of local tax law.

Then there's language, perhaps the

most impressive half-skill to have. To dance confidently across French sayings, to pronounce Italian dishes mellifluously and, when wandering through Spain, to say 'un poquito Español' when asked if you speak the native tongue, is a truly enviable talent to have.

When it comes to wine, 'un poquito Español', in the form of tempranillo, is just as important in a modern drinking repertoire. The Spanish red grape variety is making itself known around the world, and for good reason.

Oh, and the pronunciation, when done right, dances off your tongue like a tango and sounds like you can half-speak the language. 'Temp-rah-nee-yo.' Never lose eye contact. Say it with confidence so it sounds like even you have got un poquito Español.

## THE SLIPSTREAM OF WONDER

L ittle things can seem very big in a small group.
      I suspect this is what makes a social group as comforting as it is constricting, as liberating as it is limiting.

But even in your own group, you can't always find your people.

Whenever I wonder about another way of living, as I often do – more out of curiosity than dissatisfaction – I take myself out of there to get some space. I have come to call this 'riding the slipstream of wonder'. On it, I travel anywhere in the world, past or present, and hang out with anyone I'm fond of, living or dead, fictional or real, to observe and discuss different ideas and ways of living.

For example, in the real world, I zoom across to other places – usually bigger cities – to give my ideas and concerns space to breathe. The order of things and range of options to choose from seems vaster. More people equals more ways of doing things, I guess. It's not just places I fly to, but time I fly through as well. Flying back in time creates endless possibilities for exploration. With such freedom I kick around Paris in the 20s and wonder if it was really All That. If I want to terrify myself I take a turn in medieval times – all those stakes and burnings make me quickly appreciate my current liberties. And I'll walk through protests and marches in which people actually fought for things – some paying with their lives, for issues we now consider basic rights – to see what it means to truly struggle.

Occasionally, I'll take a turn about the room with Mr Darcy and others from the landed gentry, just to see if I could keep up with the conversation and to appreciate that, as pressured as things seem now, they could always be much more repressive.

And I love to fly into seminal moments of history, like that instant when, exploring the Galapagos Islands on his ship *The Beagle*, Charles Darwin thought for the first time, with more anxiety than exhilaration, that maybe – just maybe – God had nothing to do with it.

Wine is an ideal slipstream along which to take such a ride, wandering and wondering, through time and place.

Can you imagine meandering around Georgia some seven thousand years ago, native and gnarly vines running wild like bush, picking some of the first grapes harvested to make wine? How wonderful to watch the early vintages. And what of the taste?

I'd definitely fly in for a long and wild all-night bacchanalia on the Aventine Hill in Rome, celebrating Bacchus's work, sweating, dancing, drinking and doing whatever else was said to occur by moonlight in honour of the god of wine around 200 BC.

I would also spend some time in the tower of Château de Montaigne in Saint-Émilion near Bordeaux where philosopher Michel de Montaigne wrote his famous essays while surrounded by harvests and civil wars.

I might even go underground and listen closely, like a doctor with a stethoscope, to see if some time after the Second World War the Earth let out a disappointed sigh when we started using chemicals on our vineyards.

Anywhere, anytime, anyone. Try it, because if you spend just five minutes letting your mind travel on the slipstream of wonder, nothing will ever seem too big or too small or even the slightest bit dull again.

## TRANSFORMATIONS

That something brilliant can come from the pain of trauma is almost impossible to believe, especially when the trauma is happening to you. But good does come from adversity. In fact, sometimes adversity is the only way to reveal something more brilliant than what it tore apart.

This, I have come to believe, is as true of people as it is of nature, as real to relationships as it is to winemaking, as important to storytelling as the story itself.

When it comes to people, it is certainly from the messes that character grows, beliefs form and dispositions are made more complex. Traumatic things transform us, but it's not always for the worst. Some of the most brilliant artists and thinkers had challenging backgrounds, unhappy childhoods or tortured minds. And what makes up the great narratives of our time but the Hero's Journey? Our greatest and most admired protagonists in stories and books throughout time became heroes because of major transformation through adversity. As they say, adversity introduces man to himself.

In nature, it seems to be the order of things.

Most mountains arise from shifting plates and major disturbances with the Earth's crust – Mount Everest is a result of India and Asia crashing into each other. Violent volcanic activity can also leave behind more than a wake of destruction: islands arise from deep-sea volcanoes, and flourishing landscapes are revealed. Sicily's Mount Etna has provided a new ecosystem of rocky volcanic soils for vines and a community to flourish.

Perhaps the most destructive natural occurrence with a positive result was the Big Bang. Even the cynics will admit it's an impressive end result.

I thought about this idea with regards to winemaking and noted the many traumas, mild and momentous, that contribute to the wondrous result of a bottle of wine. When I looked into it through this lens I realised that, as romanticised as it is, winemaking is a veritable battleground.

In the vineyard, in addition to the geological traumas that created the various soil types and slopes, the best vines are raised in an environment of tough love. The best quality fruit comes from vines grown in poor soils and often in marginal climates; the tough conditions force the vines to dig deeper and work harder to produce fewer but more intensely flavoured grapes.

Throughout the growing season, vines are ruthlessly pruned, held back and trellised to ensure the instinct to go wild, climb and flourish is curbed. It seems mean, but this training ensures the desired amount of control, ripeness, yield and management.

Winemaking only begins when the fruit starts its transformation from grapes to wine; in this epic tale, the grape is the hero, and winemaking its journey.

When you are aware of it, it is everywhere – transformation paving the way for something new and beautiful. And it's a nice reminder, when faced with an ordeal – personal or otherwise – that it's just the world doing what it has always done; making us into a better version of what we were before.

## THE HERO'S JOURNEY

IT IS THOUGHT WINE WAS 'INVENTED' (WELL, CAME ABOUT)
WHEN SPLIT OR DAMAGED GRAPES MIXED WITH THE YEAST
PRESENT NATURALLY.

The fermentation process happens when yeast, sometimes natural, sometimes added, eats the sugar, converting it into alcohol, emitting carbon dioxide as a by-product. This is one step in the larger winemaking process known as vinification. The other steps, which vary for white, red or rosé winemaking, include:

1. Destemming – If necessary, this process separates the grapes from the stems. Some winemakers prefer grapes with the stems to impart quite particular herbal characters.

2. Crushing – This is the process of breaking the skins of the grapes to let the juice run out. This is what people are doing when they stomp the grapes in half barrels.

3. Fermentation and maceration – While fermenting, the juice also extracts and leaches colour and tannins from the skins of the grapes. This gives the wine colour, structure and complexity and can be done for just a few hours or days, depending on the desired amount in the end product.

4. Pressing – Like squeezing a teabag, this is to separate the crushed grapes and skins from the wine.

5. Maturation – Wines are matured in either oak or neutral containers, such as stainless steel, to soften the wines or extract oak characters and flavours into the wine.

6. Bottling — After maturation, the wines are made ready for bottling, a process which can include stabilisation, fining and filtering so that all remaining sediments from winemaking are removed. Then they are bottled.

'I could tell you my adventures — beginning from this morning ... but it's no use going back to yesterday, because I was a different person then.'

—*Lewis Carroll,* Alice's Adventures in Wonderland

# TRAVEL

I 've always said that if I had children they would be geniuses, and beautiful, and exist only in the 100th percentile of everything, and that a great way to help them learn would be to choose a historical journey from their curriculum and take my multilingual little gifts on it to learn about it first hand.

Clearly I don't have children, otherwise I would know they are quite hard to travel with and about as likely to be interested in wandering a desert following the route of Genghis Khan as they would be in proactively writing a schedule of their weekly chores.

You know, it's lucky I don't have kids, as I suspect this is actually *my* dream – if you take out Genghis and insert wine, that is.

There's no limit to the amount of travel you can do for wine, and the wine atlas of the world is expanding; it will be a long time before your bucket list is done. Frankly, I'm happy knowing there is no end to the list because, as long as you breathe air, there will always be something new in the world of wine.

Wine is a magical lens through which to see the world. As for choosing where? Well, the world is your oyster.

My list keeps growing; here are some adventures.

*'I haven't been everywhere, but it's on my list.'*

—Susan Sontag

## ❧ TASTING NOTES ❧

❧ You might like to work through the wine list, starting at the top with Champagne, then move on to the aromatic white wines from Alsace, Austria and Germany, working on through the middle of the list to heavier whites such as chardonnay from Burgundy, Australia or the Napa Valley. From here, move on to lighter reds — Italy and New Zealand perhaps — and then to the big reds of South Australia, Bordeaux and Spain. Some decades later, you'll find yourself in the Douro Valley of Portugal or the flatlands of Rutherglen, Australia, sipping a heady fortified wine, replete.

❧ Or maybe you're more of a classics person? You could work through a sort of 'Try Before You Die' list, having your senses moved in Piedmont, Tuscany, Burgundy and Bordeaux.

❧ Maybe you like the road less travelled. Head to the countries whose wine industries are emerging, like Slovenia, Romania, Bulgaria, Serbia and Croatia — places reawakening and transforming after years of distraction.

❧ Or perhaps head to the New World to countries like Australia, the United States and New Zealand, where the landscapes and diversity of wines, varieties and winemaking styles are wide open to possibility.

❦ Persia (ok, Iran then) would be a great journey to see where the oldest evidence of wine is and to visit the town of Shiraz.

❦ Greece would be a great trip, to learn where the Cult of Dionysus was celebrated and to experience the wine industry renaissance that Greece is embracing right now.

❦ I'd like to head to the African continent for safari, wilderness and animals, and South African wines.

❦ France is a must, because no narrative on wine is complete without it: wars, religion, tradition and, many would agree, the best wines in the world.

❦ Argentina would be on the list. I'd slide into some cowboy boots, pack a hand-crafted steak knife, and ride close to the earth on horseback through the vineyards of Mendoza.

❦ Italy is of course essential, for the great red wines Chianti and barolo, the emerging southern regions and for every other sensory pleasure that has moved people in that country over the centuries.

❦ Spain, for its range of climates, wines and food. From the rugged northern corner of Galicia, the food and wine of San Sebastian, the famed Rioja and Ribera del Duero regions, and the Mediterranean areas of the south and east, all the while enjoying the diversity of flavours that change as the geography does.

❦ And of course, a journey that's hard to tire of, the great Australian road trip. Taking the coast roads or the in-roads, from the Great Southern and Margaret River regions in the corner of Western Australia, across the red dirt to South Australia and its famed vineyards of the Clare Valley, McLaren Vale, the Barossa and others, across the border to Victoria and the maritime Mornington Peninsula, the famed Yarra Valley and the ancient soils of Heathcote, up north to New South Wales, through its hot dry middle and out to the Hunter Valley. At least, that's a start.

# TRENDS

I t's the human condition to obsess about everything but the present. What we're really interested in is the romance of the past and the possibilities that shine so brightly in the future. It's interesting to think of wine and drink trends: the past, the present and the future. As I scan the montage of my drinking life, I am surprised at how many drink fads I have endured.

Take cocktails, for instance. A decade ago we had the ultra-glamorous cosmopolitans that we bought to match our Manolo Blahniks, and we actually convinced ourselves that we'd loved them well before *Sex and the City* made them popular. Or how about the South American–inspired caprioskas, those gorgeous, heady drinks that took three days to make and three weeks' work to pay for? How swiftly we ditched them when we realised they took that long to make – sorry, *muddle* – Every. Single. Time. And then there's cider. Ever since the casually cool Kate Moss was spotted at Glastonbury in hot pants and designer gumboots clutching a pint of cider, plenty have followed suit.

These drinks were all being guzzled at a boom time in our history when we were keen to flaunt our wealth. Of course, wine has gone through the same cycle as well.

Chardonnay suffered a fall from the A-list in recent years, her only fault being her flexibility and willingness to dance to any winemaking song that was played for her. Happily, it is these very virtues that will help her endure and re-form (as she is already doing, Madonna-like) after the fall.

Sauvignon blanc has had a bit of a time lately. There she was, going about her lovely way, being the subtle, light, drink-now wine with the lovely French heritage – then *boom!* The New World took her to places her French cousins never imagined.

Red wines have been affected too. Recent pop culture has driven a small and now fading fad where wine drinkers suddenly noted the complexity of pinot noir, which incidentally was now the only red they liked, at the same time that they turned their noses up at merlot. That's showbiz. And of course, the most notable shift in red wines, to big and intense styles, has led us to now wonder if they were perhaps too big, at the expense of something more important.

I take note of the current shifts in wine, and wonder how this will affect the future.

Right now, we're talking about a sense of place, natural wine-making, hand-crafting our wine, and listening to nature. We're also finding joy in the Old World and its artisan ways, native varieties and loyalty to itself. This is the turning, the change, the reaction to the heady, showy, badge-hungry days of the past.

I wonder what's coming next and if, just by thinking this, it means the tide is turning again.

### ❦   TASTING NOTES   ❦

❦   Trends are towards more artisanal winemaking. Many winemakers are going back to viticulture and winemaking that uses less of the controlling technology than we have in recent decades. This means less interventionist winemaking in all its forms: organic, biodynamic and natural.

❦  Despite a trend towards increased alcohol levels (whether for reasons of fashion, or climate change), we are now starting to see an interest in lower level of alcohol in wines, whether they are wines that come lower in alcohol naturally, through viticultural management, or through technology during winemaking.

❦  I wonder if, as seems to be happening in other areas of consumption, those things that constitute 'premium', the reason we are willing to pay more for something, will be based on 'good' values rather than those pertaining to luxury, as in days gone by. Such values as fair trade, sustainable winegrowing practices and environmental friendliness will be considered worth paying more for.

❦  There are also country-specific trends: in Australia a range of new varieties are being experimented with, a renaissance of the Greek wine industry and focus on indigenous varieties is happening, the emergence of southern Italian varieties continues to gain momentum, and, although not exactly new, the 'grower champagne' trend in Champagne (of growers keeping some of their own fruit and making their own champagne, rather than sending it all to the big champagne houses) should continue.

# TRUTH

*In vino veritas.* 'In wine there is truth.' So said Pliny the Elder, the Roman philosopher and naturalist from thousands of years ago. I think he says it as a warning: you know, that the truth also comes out against your better judgement.

We all know this to be true. But even still, it takes a bit to sink in,

## PLINY THE ELDER

Pliny the Elder was a Roman naturalist and author who wrote the encyclopaedia *Naturalis Historia* (*Natural History*) for the Emperor Titus. The thirty-seven books that made up the work included at least two books dedicated to wine and viticulture.

Amongst his discussions, Pliny concluded that it was the place and site that determined the quality of the wine more than the variety. However, his most famous conclusion about wine is that if you drink too much, you will also speak the truth.

*especially* if you've been drinking wine, which is odd, given this is really the whole point of him saying it. But no matter how much I know this to be true, or how many times I make the mistake, it occasionally slips my mind if I am truly revelling in the pleasures of a nice bottle of wine.

I once knew someone who was much better at managing her wine than I, one of those self-disciplined types whose watchful presence made it feel like there was a headmistress at the party. She seemed to wait for others to enjoy a glass or two of wine while refraining herself, and then drilled the giddy-with-wine-delight people, myself included, for information.

At first I thought all her questions were flattering. 'Gosh,' I thought, 'I must be quite interesting.' There I was, being fed wine and *bla bla bla*–ing like a small child with a face full of red cordial.

Despite the loveliest of dinners and most interesting of conversations, I'd leave feeling unsettled. It took several dinners for me to realise that the communication offerings – and the wine consumption – were somewhat lopsided.

Then one day, she too imbibed, and let a few things slip. 'I'll find out,' she said, 'I love to trick things out of people. It's my specialty.'

And just like that – the truth.

Pliny was right.

Well, Pliny and François de La Rochefoucauld when he said, 'Moderation is an ostentatious proof of our strength of character.'

# VARIETIES

Grapes to make wine are different from table grapes or drying grapes. Most wines in the world today are made from the European wine vine, *Vitis vinifera*, of which there are more than ten thousand varieties, ensuring you'll never be bored.

When friends ask about different wine varieties, I sometimes use a comparison to something more familiar, like apples, to help them understand that different grape varieties are just like different apple varieties. Just as 'Granny Smith', 'Ribston pippin', 'jonathan', 'Golden Delicious' and 'Blenheim Orange' are just different names for different types of apples, so 'chardonnay', 'riesling', 'cabernet sauvignon', 'vermentino' and 'shiraz' are just different names for different varieties of grapes.

Each variety has its own set of conditions in which it likes to grow, and its own possibilities for what it can smell and taste like, which is why some varieties are only grown in some areas of the world and why some people can know what a riesling, for example, will generally taste like. Much

### THE BEST OF BOTH WORLDS

Hermaphrodite vines probably came about over thousands of years as vines were selected for their productivity. Vineyards were once made up of male and female vines and when the male vines didn't produce fruit, they were ripped out — which subsequently caused issues for the female vines. The hermaphrodite ones that were still producing fruit were cultivated.

of the discussion about wine is around this: how good the wine is, given what the variety's potential is.

Why this even matters is a whole other discussion, but my friends take this nugget of information away, seemingly satisfied – or perhaps just happy to have learned something more about apples. ('Sorry, *what* sort of pippins?') But truth be told, I am not sure if I'm being honest with them. Perhaps I am being misleading by making things too simple; kind of like telling someone that people are easy to understand because there are only two types: men and women.

***

## VINTAGE

A friend of mine knew a winemaker who had a winery about an hour out of Melbourne. It was good timing because vintage (or harvest, as it's called in other parts of the world) had started and, if I was game, I could go up for a weekend and help out. Just wear something old, he said, and don't worry – they'd show me what to do.

I walked into the new winery, set on a slope in the Strathbogie Ranges, on a bright and bracing autumn day. 'Slaves!' said Sticks, with his hands in the air as if he had won a bet. I was told that not only was he a giant ('Sticks' is his nickname because he is as tall as a sequoia), he was also a good-humoured kind of bloke, so I thought he was joking.

I was quickly absorbed into the industry of vintage. I remember music echoing through the winery, sometimes competing against the sounds of machine presses and crushers; the gushing purple wine – in a stream that was fire-hose thick – pumping over a tank of crushed grapes as vivid a purple as I can remember; scary-looking steel presses; and the tension that built as crates of grapes wobbled in on forklifts; and the urgent beeping of the moving trucks that added to the momentary pressure. The smells were bold and organic and belied the industrial set-up of the winery: pungent yeast, fresh grapes, cedar and oak. People spoke of night shifts and of sleeping at the winery. It felt part adventure, part festival.

That night at the local homestead, the winemakers and cellar hands – of which I was now one for at least another day – ate dinner together. The wine was the most important dish, its needs more considered than those of the guests. I just listened as they spoke of it, made space for it and matched everything to it.

The slog continued the next day as I stood on a plank across an open fermenter, willing my waning and shaking arms to push a foot-deep cap of grape skins back down into the fermenting broth. And I sat for what seemed like hours on a crate at the door in the base of a tank, holding a hose the girth of my leg that pumped wine back over grape skins. It was like cleaning out the tea leaves in a giant's teapot.

In between these jobs, I swept excess water into drains in the winery floor as fast as it came back in. My clothes became wet and sticky with grape juice, and the creases in my hands were high-lighted with the dark stain of crushed grapes.

Late in the afternoon of my second day I was sitting on the walkway of an outdoor tank that stood taller than a house. Set on the hill, it felt much, much higher, as though I was suspended in mid-air over the wide, open valley. The sun was soft and the shadows long. Looking across the land peppered with large grey boulders, I felt I had just stepped into something that had me so curious I didn't even know where to begin to understand it.

That afternoon I got a ride back to the city. With wine-stained hands and still wearing my work clothes, which were marbled with red wine, I felt like a soldier returning from a mission. I was proud of the evidence of vintage, even though the stains seemed silly in inner-city Melbourne as trams rattled past and people spilled from Sunday sessions at the pub.

As I walked the last blocks home I made a detour to the local bottle shop, determined to make whatever had just happened to me last a little longer. Scanning the rows and bottles with little idea but the greatest of intentions, I made the most generous offer I could – I handed over my last $20 and bought the most expensive bottle of wine that I had ever owned.

## 🍇 TASTING NOTES 🍇

🍇 Vintage, or harvest, depending on where you are in the world, is the time when the grapes are picked and the winemaking process begins.

🍇 Vintage starts in autumn, but its exact start time is largely determined by the ripeness of the grapes: when the winegrowers determine that it has hit that sweet spot where acid has gone down enough and sugars have risen — at least as best as can be, given the vintage's conditions, variety, region and the style of wine they're after.

🍇 For many, vintage is a sort of addictive rush — the frenzy and drama keep them coming back. As one winemaker once said to me, 'This is it. It's when the wine is born, it's the beginning of life.'

## WAITER'S FRIENDS

Seamlessly opening a bottle of wine with a waiter's friend is one of those small but important skills cool people pull off without thinking about – like actors in old movies lighting a cigarette with a swipe of a match on their boot. Other small but important knacks include opening a beer bottle with a coin, and flipping something in a fry pan while sipping wine and holding eye contact with someone else.

I don't know where you get taught these small but important skills. It reminds me of when I was, for about a minute and a half, a girl guide. I don't know why it was offered – such traditions were not really the thing for women in my family – and I don't know why I said yes. Maybe because my friend was a boy scout and he did cool things for badges, like camping and hiking and making fires and stuff like that.

My only memory of being taught such skills was being asked to fry an egg. There I was in a suburban kitchen in a dull brown dress, cooking, while my friend was off learning to tie knots, build a fire and make rafts. Why was I stuck frying an egg for someone called Brown Owl? I hear it's changed a lot and girls can now be scouts. That'd be right. I bet these days you can even get a badge for removing a cork with a waiter's friend.

## ❦ Tasting notes ❦

### How to remove a wine cork with a waiter's friend:

❦ Open the small blade and slice the top off the foil. Pull it off.

❦ Hide the knife and pull down the corkscrew, place it bulls-eye in the middle of the cork, then twist. Be sure to steer the corkscrew straight down the centre so you don't run it out of the side of the cork.

❦ Once it's in, pull the notched lever down and lock it onto the side to lever the cork out. Eye contact with your guests while doing this helps instill confidence in your abilities.

### How to remove a cork without a waiter's friend:

❦ Peel off the cap and push the cork down into the bottle with a fat texta or something. I know, but it's the best you've got and you forgot the corkscrew.

❦ You can also stick a serrated knife in the cork and pull it out that way.

❦ Hammer nails into the cork and pull them out with the other side of the hammer.

❦ Or even wrap the wine in a towel and knock it against a brick wall — but that just sounds like trouble to me.

You might also consider going back to Girl Guides to learn how to provision for camping properly.

# WIND

I t's a bit of a trick, wind, because it's not hard, like a mountain, but it can be as large; it's not wet like the ocean, but it can carry that much water; it's not productive like a plant, but it can broadcast a plant's seeds; it's not mellifluous like music, but it does come in waves; and it's not transport like a yacht, but it can propel passengers thousands of miles around the world.

I was once taken down the front of a yacht – I hadn't been sailing long – where I was taught to watch for wind so I could warn the crew of sudden gusts: helpful when racing and when trying to balance a glass of wine. 'How can I see wind?' I asked, but there it was: small clusters of patterns flickering across the ocean, like a ripple left by passing yet invisible birds.

Once you learn to see wind as a thing, you can't see it as anything else – watch it rustling leaves on trees, moving people's hair, making the surface of water busy and snapping sheets on a clothesline.

Every day since time began, wind has helped to shape the world, influencing where its animals flourished, how and where civilisations developed and roads ran; wind has helped to shape the surface of the Earth, is responsible for some of the most magnificent shapes, the desert basins and the spines of dunes, that mark the landscape the world over.

The trade winds, the prevailing winds found near the tropics, have been relied upon for exploration, trade (as the name would suggest) and travel for centuries. For sailors, with only natural power to rely on, these were the highways. Wind was fortune: the doldrums are those areas where the prevailing winds are calm or non-existent – hence, when we say we're in them, things aren't going well.

Migratory birds rely on wind for their annual pilgrimage across hemispheres. The bar-tailed godwit, known to make the longest migratory journey of any bird, relies on no less than five different wind systems in the Pacific to make its non-stop 11,500-kilometre journey from Alaska to New Zealand. Without the wind, the journey would not be possible.

Some winds are so predictable in certain parts of the world, with such distinct personalities, that they have been given names – the Santa Ana winds of Southern California, the hurricane force of the Zonda in Argentina, the Fremantle Doctor of Western Australia, the mistral of France and sirocco of North Africa and Southern Europe – all of which affect winegrowing regions in those countries.

Wind in viticulture has benefits just as it has complications. Like in sailing, whether or not wind is a good thing in winegrowing is all a matter of degree.

## ❦   Tasting notes   ❦

❦ In addition to the tempering effect of the ocean, wind helps moderate and keep temperatures cool along coastal and maritime wine regions.

❦ Where vineyards are susceptible to humidity, airflow helps dry wet vines and prevent mildew building up and creating rot. This is why in some vineyards near tropical areas, you can see vines hung on high pergola systems – the viticultural equivalent of lifting the hem of your dress to let your legs cool.

❦ Wind, often generated by man-made windmills in frost-prone areas, can also help prevent the frost that occurs when cold, still air collects and damages young buds. When the wind keeps the air moving, the fog cannot settle.

❦ On the downside, hot dry winds dehydrate vineyards, and heavy consistent winds are a problem for flowering. And in places where the wind can be harsh, vines adapt in other ways. On the Greek island of Santorini, vines are coiled like ropes close to the ground to protect themselves against the harsh Mediterranean winds.

# WINE TALK

I n and of itself, wine is not that difficult a concept – we accept far more complex things every day without raising an eyebrow. What *is* a complex thing about wine is that there are so many thousands of details, and we insist on talking about all of them.

I suspect it's too late in the game to suggest there might be more pleasure gained by relaxing this idea, but when someone asked me recently what all the talk was about, I was curious enough with the question to try to puzzle it out. It's a good one: what *is* all the talk about?

Well, it starts out with a grape variety (like chardonnay). Each variety has certain characteristics that are innate to it, such as its colour, flavour, aroma, and how it likes to grow and where it can grow.

As the variety goes through its life cycle, it changes. Some of these changes happen naturally, some randomly and others happen at the hand of humans; and the effects can be anything between transcendent and catastrophic.

More specifically, some of the points for discussion include:

- Where the variety comes from – Which country is it from and, within this, which region? Is it a good one? Fashionable? Traditional or modern?

- How the variety is grown – Is it done organically, chemically, controversially, experimentally or somewhere more middle-of-the-road?

- What the wine's pedigree is – Who made it? Is this the product of a big corporate family with lots of money? Or a small artisan who's a little kooky? Something more stable and in-between?

- Whether the wine ages well – What choices were made throughout its life to impact or influence how well it ages? Choices include the amount of human intervention in winemaking, the choice of barrels, and the amount of time the wine was left alone.

- Whether the wine is good – How good did the wine turn out to be? Did it meet expectations or take a different turn?

- What it would be good to pair with – What flavours does it match or complement, if any?

- Whether the wine is successful – Did the wine win awards? Was it written about favourably? Is this reputation justified? Was the judging of it involved in any scandal?

You see, when you look at it like that, you can see it's just like a living thing, moving through its life cycle with a lot of judgement and commentary about its particular choices and their consequences.

Still confused?

Replace the word 'variety' or 'wine' in that list with 'person'.

Not so weird is it? It's what we talk about every day. And, given that, it's no wonder we're all confused.

## WINE TEMPERATURE

A heat haze shimmers from the dry earth, a sweat bead slides from your hairline down your neck, words come slowly, birds fall silent with exhaustion, the air is dry, the sun high. You sip your wine in the hope of relief, but it's lukewarm. Instead of cooling you, it's like a tepid mouthful of alcohol. You seek relief by sliding your hand in the cool of the ice bucket, full of chilled water and clinking ice. You grab a cube and look longingly at your wine glass. Yes, go ahead – it's ok to put a cube of ice in your glass. Wine is about refreshment, and that means a cool, refreshing wine is better than a lukewarm one. I probably wouldn't suggest the same relaxed attitude with your most precious wine, but then you probably wouldn't be drinking it in the searing hot sun ... would you? No, you wouldn't.

### ❧ Tasting notes ❧

#### The temperature of a wine has a large impact on how it tastes.

❧ In general, sparkling, white and rosé wines should be served chilled and red wines at room temperature. Variations exist within this.

❧ If you think about wine along a continuum of shades of white to yellow, through to light red to deep and dark purple, the lighter and whiter your wine, the colder it should be, warming up to room temperature for the darkest and heaviest red wines. The exception to this rule is rosé, which should always be served ice cold.

❧ The fastest way to chill wine is to empty a tray or two of ice blocks into an ice bucket, put the bottle in, and then fill the bucket with water; this ensures the bottle has more surface area surrounding and cooling your wine.

❧ If your red wine is too cold, hold the bowl of the glass in your hand and use the heat from your hard to warm it up a little. As you do, more aromas will be released and the wine will appear more generous.

# WINE'S SPIRIT

I walked the hour from the village to the winery along a quiet, narrow road that wound through vines dangling the last of the season's fruits. Deep pinkish pinot gris and gewürztraminer bunches drooped lazily from their vines. It was late autumn, and the leaves were tingeing from lush green to yellow and orange. Come winter, I was told, this road would be snowed over.

As I walked, I tried to imagine what it was like in medieval times – when walking outside of the city walls, wandering alone between villages and vineyards, was a dangerous and courageous thing to do.

Although I had come to taste wines, I wanted to taste something else: a version of life that I was curious about. A quiet calling to something that felt entirely real yet utterly invisible; it was as much about being a writer as wanting to be free from a life of settling down. I wanted to be able to be curious for a living. I had a romantic idea of what this might be like, wandering and wondering, travelling and writing – but what if it was only that? An unrealistic and imagined idea?

The only tangible thing I had, by way of explanation, was to say I was going to taste wines – but it was a spirited life I wanted to taste. Such tastings were in some way a road test to see if my curiosity for wine could indeed become something more.

My boots crunched on the gravel driveway as I approached the large ancient convent that now housed a winery. Pots of pink geraniums and a row of pink roses flashed against the ruddy cream walls. The grand building was surrounded by vineyards and set against the folds of the lush Vosges Mountains. Grey clouds hovered, making the scene both beautiful and dramatic.

The old Alsatian monastery was built in the 800s, and the domaine was established by monks in the 1600s. It has been in the hands of the current family for over a century and is now run by the matriarch and her two daughters. I'd heard a whisper that the matriarch's late husband was laid to rest among the vineyards.

'Bonjour!' The door swept open, and my host, the tall and graceful elder of the two daughters, greeted me, then looked beyond me, frowning at the rainclouds. It was late harvest – when the grapes that are allowed to ripen longer to make the sweeter wines are picked. Earlier that morning it had rained and the pickers were sent home. 'It is nature, what can you do?' she asked, holding out her arm, gesturing for me to come inside.

I adore the way winegrowers talk of and eyeball nature like a familiar and often belligerent elder. It's as lifelong and irrefutable a relationship as the one with yourself.

The estate was farmed biodynamically – a philosophy that treats the farm as a self-sustaining and interlinked universe. The wines of the domaine were famed for their purity, quality and elegance.

Inside, the tasting parlour was a small and beautiful wood-panelled room on the ground floor. In the middle of the room was an antique table, upon which sat some wine glasses, two spittoons and three tall, elegant Alsatian wine bottles.

The first wines, varieties traditional to the region – pinot blanc, riesling and pinot noir – were at once engaging. There was freshness and acidity, energy and balance and an alluring prettiness with depth. These were familiar enough descriptors, but there seemed to be something else going on.

We continued through more whites, on to rieslings and gewürztraminers from different sites.

These wines had as many rooms of flavour to explore as the old monastery. I tried to capture it with detailed notes, but it was like trying to embrace a ghost. Where other perfectly good wines had immaculate flat horizon lines, these wines seemed to undulate and flow over hills and folds, across Earth and into infinity. My notes and mind began to wander and I noticed the small and delicate details of the room – the floral upholstery on the old wooden couch, the pattern on the rug, the vase of pink roses and the cluster of grape flies that hovered over them like a handful of confetti that wouldn't land. I saw people and faces in the framed portraits and photos that seemed to span centuries.

I had a sudden urge to ask my host questions about life. What did she know of life, of love? What were the universal truths, and did she have the answers? Only shyness prevented me from giving my curiosity voice.

We moved on to rieslings from the famous grand cru Schlossberg vineyard, one of the most esteemed vineyards in Alsace. Yes, they had exotic aromas, floral and blossom, a line of acidity, and wonderful minerality, but there was more than that. They were more than beautiful, they were transcendent.

These wines made me feel like I was being led underground and let in on nature's secrets.

There were no tasting descriptors for this: what was it?

I tried to take notes, but to say 'floral notes and a long acid line' seemed as apt as describing van Gogh's *The Starry Night* as 'a painting of yellow stars on a dark-blue sky'. The wines were made up of one seamless wave of flavour after another. I wanted to say the wines had clarity – but of what? This wasn't familiar, but I knew it to be pure.

I looked out the large parlour window, across the gravel entrance, the vineyards, the grey clouds, and to the hills and beyond. I wanted to run thrashing through the vines till I was out of breath, falling to the earth, panting with joy.

My mind wandered to history, to kings and revolutions, to natural occurrences happening tens of millions of years ago – faults buckling the Earth and making the patchwork of terroir. I searched for, but I could not find, the beginning.

How can this be just wine?

The idea of spirit – in wine and life – is a contentious and curious one: contentious because it's hard to prove one way or the other, and curious for precisely the same reason. Yet comments such as 'It's hard to explain, but there's something else there', and 'It's more than wine, it's life' are often whispered.

Was this it?

I was reminded of an essay called *The Force of Spirit*, by Scott Russell Sanders, where he searches for a name for this universal force: 'This power is larger than life, although it contains life. It's tougher than love, although it contains love … No name is large enough to hold this power, but of all the inadequate names the one that comes to me now is spirit … I cannot understand the world, cannot understand my life, without appealing to the force of spirit,' wrote Sanders. 'The Latin word for breath is *spiritus*, which also means courage, air, and life.'

My host asked what I thought of the wines. I turned away toward the window again, to compose myself. Were I alone, I might have wept.

It didn't matter anymore whether the joy was real or in my imagination – there was no difference, and the wines were part of something much larger. Courage. Air. Life.

What did I think of the wines? They were beautiful, but more than that, they seemed to legitimise the magnificent and the invisible.

It was there and then, in an ancient monastery in France, that I looked out the window across the vines and knew it was possible and perfectly fine for wine to be my lodestar. Not only would it be fine, it might also be breathtaking.

'The White Rabbit put on his
spectacles. "Where shall I begin,
please, your Majesty?" he asked.
"Begin at the beginning," the King
said gravely, "and go on till you
come to the end: then stop."'

—*Lewis Carroll,* Alice's Adventures
in Wonderland

# AFTERWORD

*Dear Dionysus,*

*No wonder you're hurting; these days, it's like you're dead.*

*I don't need to tell you another vintage has gone by with not so much as thanks, let alone a harvest festival in your honour.*

*How does this even happen?*

*There you were, son of Zeus and the reason wine existed. I mean, wine was your gig. Helios had sun, Apollo had light, Poseidon had the sea and you were in charge of wine. And oh, oh dear god Dionysus, how well you did it. The vintages, the fruit, the wine, the aromas and tastes, it was all you.*

*Remember the festivals? Those were the days, weren't they? Before and after every harvest there was so much fanfare and celebration, so many dancers and parades, the beating drums and sacrificial bulls, ladies in their little fawn-skin skirts and men in theirs.*

*It wasn't just the parties – although they were quite something. When you really started to gain popularity there was the open theatre about you and your life – by, who was that again? Euripides? – I mean, seriously. Talk about the halcyon days of yore.*

*What really gets me about it all is that you played a fair and open hand, too. You showed them the downside to drunkenness and debauchery, warning them about the thoughtlessness and rage that come with drinking too much wine. That took real honesty and courage.*

*Yet still, the redundancy.*

*If you had to point your fennel staff at anyone, I guess you could blame the Romans. They took a perfectly well-run festival that had been celebrated for centuries and turned it into the wild and mystic Bacchanalia. Parties during the night? A secret guest list? Nudity and conspiracy? Yeah, right. Those guys ruined it for everyone.*

*Well, maybe they can't be blamed entirely for your demise. Over the years, the religious types with their rules about how people should behave and the scientists with their information about how wine was made also had something to do with it.*

*You won't believe what's happening now – wine is made all over the world, quality is better than ever and they're not crediting you for a single bit. Your long-term strategy has been rolled out and stolen by people claiming to be pioneers and innovators of wine.*

*You know who they give thanks to now? Winemakers! And in quite a congratulatory manner, too, constantly awarding themselves trophies and medals the minute they so much as bottle your hard work. There are even hall of fame awards bestowed after ten to fifteen years in the game. You put in a good couple of thousand years and what do you get?*

*Ok, sure, they talk about you in art and Greek mythology, and there are paintings and statues of you, not to mention a number of wine bars and businesses adorned with your name. Yet still, no real thanks, not like in the old days.*

*Maybe it's changing. Winemakers are starting to wonder if something other than their hard work is at play, but they're slow on the uptake. You know what they say it is? Terroir. 'It's just the mystery of wine,' they say, as if that mystery is not you at work.*

*No wonder you're angry and you lashed out with those difficult vintage conditions: hail, frost, rain and disease. The other gods say it's the anger talking and that you need to move on, but I see they're just cries for help. You're hurting.*

*I know this is probably hard, me bringing this up, especially as you asked me to stop writing last vintage. 'Let it scab,' you said, before storming off, sprinkling random vineyards with downy mildew and phylloxera as you went.*

*It's just that every time vintage comes around, as I watch vineyards erupt in rows of autumnal colours, as the grapes fatten and ripen before being plucked by winegrowers rejoicing at another harvest, I get a little melancholy that you're not getting the credit.*

*I just want you to know that I still believe in you, Dionysus. I know you're still the god of wine and, as soon as this vintage is done, I'll be giving thanks for your hard work – fawn-skin skirt and all.*

*–Andrea Frost*

# INDEX

# ACKNOWLEDGEMENTS

MY HEARTFELT THANKS:

To Tony Birch, for the best education I never had. To my friends and 'tiger mothers' Sophie Torney and Lorna Hendry; to Max Allen for generously reading and commenting on an early version of this book. To The Gang for the cellar door tastings and every wine we've shared in between. To Cable Daniel-Dreyfus for the salons gone and to come. To Todd Abbott for our loose literary discussions and lovely nights out. To Erez Gordon for the early push, the conversations and because we agreed I'd thank you when. To Meaghan O'Kane for our very special walks and talks among the gardens. To the many, many wine industry friends who have helped to keep wine fun and interesting along the way, including Michael Hill Smith, Angie Bradbury and Stuart Gregor. To the Triple 0. To Andrew Jefford for the generous comments about this book. To Fred Pawle for reading and encouraging since way back when. To Kate Goodman for keeping tastings fun. To Dan Sims for the boundless enthusiasm. To the readers of my blog and twitter friends who have shown support and encouragement, without which, I might have wondered quietly. To Scarlet Ribbon and crew for getting us all across the Tasman Sea. To Writers Victoria for the use of Glenfern during periods of writing this book. To the wineries that provided the back drop for many of the stories in *Through a Sparkling Glass* including; Domaine Zind-Humbrecht ('Ageing'), the Faller family at Domaine Weinbach ('Wine's Spirit'), Pierrot Le Fou ('Alsace'), Marie-Noëlle Rainon-Henriet from Henriet-Bazin, ('A Lovely Cuvee') and Nicholas Rainon from Oenovasion ('A Minerality Lesson'). To the wineries I forgot to mention. To Steven. To Ava. To Dee Clements. To The Frost Family. To the tireless efforts of the editing and publishing team of *Through a Sparkling Glass* including Fran Berry, Rose Michael and Allison Hiew. To the many, many dear friends I have enjoyed – and will continue to enjoy – the wonders of wine with … and for everything else, DC.